SKILL FOR
BATTLE
THE ART OF SPIRITUAL WARFARE

SKILL FOR BATTLE
THE ART OF SPIRITUAL WARFARE

Unless otherwise noted, all Scripture quotations are taken from the *King James Version of the Bible.*

Scripture quotations marked (NLT) are taken from the *Holy Bible, New Living Translation*, copyright © 1996, 2004. Used by permission of Tyndale House Publishers, Inc., Wheaton, Illinois 60189. All rights reserved.

Scripture quotations marked (TNIV) are taken from the *Holy Bible, Today's New International Version*®. Copyright © 2001, 2005 by International Bible Society®. Used by permission. All rights reserved worldwide.

Scripture quotations marked (AMP) are taken from the *Amplified*® *Bible,* copyright © 1954, 1958, 1962, 1964, 1965, 1987 by The Lockman Foundation. Used by permission. (www.Lockman.org)

Copyright © 2009 by Dr. David R. Williams

ISBN 0-938020-77-3

First Printed 2009

Cover Design by Timothy Henley

DECAPOLIS

Printed in the United States of America

OTHER BOOKS BY DAVE WILLIAMS

TABLE OF CONTENTS

SECTION 3: THE JEZEBEL SPIRIT

SECTION 4: SATAN'S TACTICS

Like no other time in history, the devil is using any tool he can find to stir up trouble and ensnare the unwary in his sin traps.

INTRODUCTION

SATAN IS IN THE WORLD

The Bible declares that the devil will work quadruple overtime in the final hours of history. Like any illegitimate ruler, he struggles to hold on to power. He knows his end draws near.

> ...Woe to the inhabiters of the earth and of the sea! for the devil is come down unto you, having great wrath, because he knoweth that he hath but a short time.
> —Revelation 12:12b

He knows all Heaven is about to crash down upon him, and he's thrashing around like a shark on the end of a fishhook—trying to take as many people as possible down to everlasting destruction with him.

Whether you like it or not, we're in a war with Satan. His evil influence permeates our society. Sin abounds and people accept as commonplace situations and events that, even a few years ago, they would have found shocking. Abortion, divorce, fornication and adultery, violence, drugs and alcohol, denial of religious freedoms, war, and many other everyday occurrences speak of a culture in crisis. The Apostle Peter wrote that believers should be self-controlled and alert.

> Be sober, be vigilant; because your adversary
> the devil, as a roaring lion, walketh about, seeking
> whom he may devour: Whom resist steadfast in
> the faith....
>
> —1 Peter 5:8–9a

Our youth are beleaguered by heavy problems. Drugs are now a regular part of youth culture. I know young people who say the pressure to use drugs is intense. Kids take drugs at the bus stop before going to school, in the bathrooms and on the playgrounds during school, and when they're hanging out together after school. One godly young man was sitting in class and one of his classmates chanted, "Oh, heroin, heroin, that's where it's at." This stoned-out kid looked at the young Christian and said, "You'd make a good burnout. Why don't you try it?"

It's interesting that drugs are very closely related to sorcery in the Bible. In fact, the word sorcery comes from the Greek word "pharmacia," which means pharmaceuticals or enchanting drugs that are used in witchcraft and occultism.

And the devil's influence doesn't stop there. Police departments now consult occultists to help them locate criminals. One local police department actually called in a spiritualist medium to help solve a crime. Major cities have been doing this for years.

Instead of seeking God's will, political leaders have been known to consult spiritualists and astrologers to find out what their next move should be. You can even get your "astrological forecast" from game machines in the foyers of many restaurants. It may seem like harmless fun, but for people who are susceptible, it can be the wedge Satan uses to invade their lives.

The level of violent crimes increases every year. I was flipping the dial on the radio recently, and I heard somebody sing, "I'm going to kill my wife. I'm going to take her life, don't try to stop me now, I've got my hands around her neck!" You might be tempted to laugh it off—it's just a song—but Jesus said the devil is a murderer (John 10:10). He's been a killer from the beginning. I wonder how many people Satan influenced through the depraved words of that song?

Like no other time in history, the devil is using any tool he can find to stir up trouble and ensnare the unwary.

GET YOUR GEAR!

Thankfully, where sin abounds, God's grace abounds all the more!

> ...But where sin increased and abounded, grace (God's unmerited favor) has surpassed it and increased the more and superabounded....
> —Romans 5:20b (AMP)

Whenever and wherever Satan is at work, God is also at work. Praise the Lord! There may be a strong influence of evil at work in the world, but the Holy Spirit is also at work; so there is a tidal wave of sinners coming to a saving relationship with Jesus Christ.

This book calls you to your battle station. It is full of sound, biblical advice; each chapter a blow to Satan's kingdom—but you must put the principles you learn into practice. Satan already fights to claim your soul. You must learn how to fight back.

Thankfully, God promises to prepare and equip us for ultimate victory.

> Bless the Lord, who is my rock. He gives me strength for war and skill for battle.

> He is my loving ally and my fortress, my tower
> of safety, my deliverer. He stands before me as a
> shield and I take refuge in him.
> —Psalm 144:1–2a (NLT)

The Bible says we're not to be ignorant of Satan's devices (2 Corinthians 2:11). This book is a manual of war. It introduces you to what the Bible says about Satan and how he tries to defeat you. You will learn the steps to recognize where he's at work and how to gain mastery over him. The basic battle plan is this:

- You must accept that Satan is real—that we are locked in a battle with him—but our victory is assured if we place our faith in Jesus and fight against the devil from a victory vantage point.
- You must be able to recognize his character and nature, his works and devices, methods and tactics. In this book, you'll learn to recognize more than two dozen of Satan's most common tactics against Christians.
- You must ostracize Satan. Banish him from your life; cast him out of your affairs.

The Bible says:

> And these signs shall follow them that believe;
> In my name shall they cast out devils....
> —Mark 16:17a

You must actively resist him and give him absolutely no ground in your life, your family, your church, your job, or your financial affairs!

THE SCRAP HEAP OF LIFE

There is a junkyard near where I grew up. I drove by it recently, and I saw beautiful late-model Cadillacs that had been totaled. They put those wrecked cars in a machine that crunched them into little square packages. They were loaded on a train and sent to be melted down. That's what the devil wants for your life. He wants to put you on the scrap heap so you'll be crushed, sent away, and melted down.

But with the help of the Bible, the Holy Spirit, and this book you'll earn your stripes in this "last days" battle. Are you willing? Let's get ready to rumble!

Dave Williams
Mount Hope Church

SECTION ONE

EXPOSING THE ENEMY

In these final hours, as we await Jesus' return, it is even more important that we understand how Satan is working in the world!

1

DO YOU BELIEVE SATAN IS REAL?

Why is it people—even some Christians—don't think the devil is real? I read of a reporter who printed up a bill of sale for the soul to transfer ownership to the devil. He went around asking people on the street to sign away the title deed to their soul in exchange for ten dollars. One out of every seven people took the deal because they didn't believe Satan is real. They believed he is a funny, harmless little man wearing red pajamas with a pointed tail and a pitchfork.

People shrug off the idea of the devil as a being who is bent on destroying mankind. But there is a devil, and he's not cute or harmless. He's a malicious destroyer. The Bible says that Jesus came to destroy the devil's works.

> **He that committeth sin is of the devil; for the devil sinneth from the beginning. For this purpose the Son of God was manifested, that he might destroy the works of the devil.**
> **—1 John 3:8**

BE STRONG

In the face of an attack, it's hard to remember the right thing to do. But Jesus gave encouragement for these times.

> **Finally, my brethren, be strong in the Lord, and in the power of his might.**
> —Ephesians 6:10

Why does Jesus urge you in this way? So you will be able to take your stand against the devil's schemes.

> **For we wrestle not against flesh and blood, but against principalities, against powers, against the rulers of the darkness of this world, against spiritual wickedness in high places.**
> —Ephesians 6:12

HOW IGNORANT ARE WE?

Evan Roberts, the leader of the great Welsh revival, said, "The devil's great purpose—for which he fights—is to keep the world in ignorance of himself, his ways, and his colleagues, and the church is taking sides with him when siding with ignorance about him."

Most churches are weak in teaching young Christians about the devil. New converts come to an altar call and get saved and don't realize why they face major attacks two days later. It's the devil! But if they haven't been warned, it can be a confusing experience.

Some well-meaning Christians say, "The devil's not worth talking about. God is in control." However, that kind of thinking ignores a good portion of the Word of God because nearly every New Testament book talks about recognizing the devil. Jesus himself spent a good deal of time casting out demons and instructing the disciples how to engage in spiritual warfare. The apostle Paul said we are not ignorant of his devices (2 Corinthians 2:11). The disciples saw how Jesus healed all who were oppressed of the devil. They understood the devices of the enemy.

In these final hours, as we await Jesus' return, it is even more important that we understand how Satan is working in the world!

The enemy is a real, intelligent creature bent on destroying you. Jesus said:

> **The thief cometh not, but for to steal, and to kill, and to destroy....**
>
> —John 10:10a

It's bad advice to say, "Ignore him, and he'll go away." While you busily ignore him, he will busily oppose every bit of positive progress in your life!

I was looking at a pamphlet published by a large medical association. It discussed the topics of depression, worry, and fear. It had cartoons of people suffering from each emotion with little clouds over their heads reading, "I'm depression. I'll depress you." Another said, "I'm fear, and I'll make you afraid." These cartoon people suffered different moods, but there was no indication of why they suffered. It did not attribute the cause of these feelings to a spiritual being. The devil was reduced to a bad feeling or hazy cloud!

That's just what Satan wants to happen. He hides his plan for you behind vague maladies that are easily reduced to non-threatening cartoons.

SATAN'S WAR MANUAL

Did you know you occupy a chapter in the devil's personal war manual? Written there is his miserable plan for your life. He's thought it out, made a strategy, taken into account your weaknesses and launched an offensive. Maybe you're aware of it; maybe you're not.

On the other hand, God loves you and has a wonderful plan for your life. You may think, "I'm safe in God. I don't have to worry about the devil." I wish that were true, but it's not. Ignoring the devil is dangerous. Just look at the life of Saul in the Old Testament.

At one time, Saul was a humble man anointed by God to be king over Israel. But the devil had a chapter about Saul in his war manual. Satan figured out his weaknesses. He had Saul's number, so to speak, and began to use Saul's jealousy to gain control.

Saul became wrapped up in self-will, lust for power, anger, and murderous thoughts. Soon he wasn't hearing from God anymore. The Spirit of God departed from him, and an evil spirit came to trouble him (1 Samuel 16:14). He went through periods of great depression. He tried to murder David and wanted his own son murdered for disobeying a simple command his son didn't know about in the first place (1 Samuel 14). Saul sold out to the devil. His family and kingdom were in turmoil, and finally he fell on his own sword and died (1 Samuel 31:1–7).

If the devil can trash the life of a man God called to be king, what could he do to you?

Sometimes it happens so slowly and subtly you don't notice. There was a twelve-year-old boy named Bobby from Houston, Texas, where there are lakes with muck so deep it acts like quicksand. If you go out too far and get caught in the muck, it pulls you under. Bobby was at the lake and saw the posted "No Swimming" sign, but he wanted shells and decided it wouldn't hurt to take his shoes off and wade a little. He didn't sink into any mud in the shallows, so he went a little further out, "just" up to his ankles, then his knees—and still the ground was solid. Soon he was up to his waist, and all of a sudden he dropped down into the muck. He screamed in terror. By the grace of God, a man heard him, threw him a rope, and pulled him out.

That's how the devil gets his claws into you. You begin by wading "just" in the shallows; then you wander a little deeper until suddenly the ground gives way and you are caught. All the while you think, "Hey, this isn't so bad. I'm doing okay. The warning signs are wrong." Then, before you can retreat, you are sucked under and destroyed. Satan wins a victory; another one "bites the dust."

You don't have to be a victim! You can learn about spiritual warfare without getting weird or obsessed with it. You can "see" with spiritual eyes and identify the devil's meddling in your life and the lives of others.

Let's find out how the spiritual world relates to you.

*The devil studies you, scrutinizes you,
and watches carefully for a way to
gain entrance into your life.*

2

GRAPPLING WITH THE SUPERNATURAL

Some things in life can only be satisfactorily explained by a spirit world coexisting with our physical world. If God would lift the veil so you could peer into the spirit world, you would forever be changed by what you saw.

A missionary working in Zambia shared this story: A man in his church got upset with another man. He thought the church didn't have the power to do anything about his offense, so he paid the local witch doctor to have a curse put on his enemy. The witch doctor made a foamy substance, like shaving cream, and smeared it on a mirror; he told the man to look in the mirror, and there he saw the face of the man he wanted cursed. The witch doctor took a razor and sliced it across the neck of the image. The man who had paid him said, "I paid you to curse the man, not to kill him." The witch doctor laughed hideously and said, "I thought I'd do the job right." That very hour the man in the mirror hemorrhaged internally and bled to death.

That may sound like a scene from a horror movie, but it's absolutely real.

A PRINCIPALITY OVER LANSING

The first time God lifted the veil for me was May 10, 1985. Before then, I thought people who had "visions" and saw "demons" were just kooky. But for a few moments, God allowed me to peer into the high places over my city, Lansing, Michigan, and it changed the way I see the world. It happened during a time of stress in our church. I was away on a trip, lying on my hotel bed, when the vision began.

In the northeast sky I saw a spiritual creature holding tens of thousands of people in a net. They flopped around like little fish, and I felt so sorry for them. I thought, "Let them go," but the creature shook his head and leered at me as if to say, "They're mine! You can't have them." I kept thinking, "Let them go," but he taunted me in return.

Then I was lifted up so I could look down into our church. I saw myself and the congregation praying with our hands lifted in warfare saying, "Principality over Lansing, we command you in the Name of Jesus Christ, loose the people!" But the demon just held the people tighter, and they became more miserable. However, as we persisted, the demon grew weaker and weaker. Finally, it seemed like God loosed angels, and the net started breaking up. People began to fall out of the net into our church. They were strange people who didn't act like Christians, but God said we had to love them.

THE RESULTS

If the vision had come and gone without anything changing at our church, I would have dismissed it. But the next week, I told the church about what I'd experienced. We embarked on twenty-one days of spiritual warfare, praying every morning and in every service against that principality over Lansing. Suddenly, the response to altar calls tripled—then quadrupled! People—who had not been to church in years—started to come.

One day, a woman wearing heavy makeup, a revealing top, and a miniskirt walked down the aisle to the altar. At first, I thought she was a man dressed like a woman because she was so overdone. Later, I learned she was a prostitute. However, she came down and accepted Jesus as her Savior. I wondered if it took. The next week, she brought two men to church with her. When I gave the altar call, she grabbed them both and marched them to the altar. She turned away from her sinful life and went on to be an outstanding member of our church!

We started seeing major results from our spiritual warfare prayers, and I knew the vision I saw was truly real, and so was the principality we were fighting.

HE IS STUDYING YOU

The devil studies you, scrutinizes you, and watches carefully for a way to gain entrance into your life. In Job 1:8, God asked Satan if he had considered God's servant Job who "is blameless and upright." The devil said (paraphrase), "You'd better believe I've considered Job." The word "consider" in Hebrew means to study and scrutinize. Satan sought a way to get a wedge between Job and God—some weakness he could exploit. He can use the most seemingly petty and insignificant sin as a stumbling block to bring down even great men and women of faith.

Just as Satan did to Job so long ago, that's what he tries to do to you today. He'll use any little thing to try to get your focus off simple devotion to Jesus. When you have a persistent problem you can't defeat by resisting temptation or speaking the Word, perhaps the devil has found a way into your life, and you need deliverance.

The things we call "moods" or "emotions," the Bible often identifies as spirits! For example, the Bible calls fear a spirit:

> For God has not given us a spirit of fear and
> timidity, but of power, love, and self-discipline.
> —2 Timothy 1:7 (NLT)

Depression was personalized and called the spirit of heaviness or despair:

> …to comfort all that mourn;
> To appoint unto them that mourn in Zion, to
> give unto them beauty for ashes, the oil of joy for
> mourning, the garment of praise for the spirit of
> heaviness….
> —Isaiah 61:2b–3a

The Bible describes lying spirits, unclean spirits, and jealous spirits:

> Now therefore, behold, the LORD hath put a
> lying spirit in the mouth of all these thy prophets,
> and the LORD hath spoken evil concerning thee.
> —1 Kings 22:23

> Jesus called his twelve disciples together and
> gave them authority to cast out evil spirits and to
> heal every kind of disease and illness.
> —Matthew 10:1 (NLT)

> Or when the spirit of jealousy cometh upon
> him, and he be jealous over his wife, and shall set
> the woman before the LORD, and the priest shall
> execute upon her all this law.
> —Numbers 5:30

Spirits are invisible, but we can see them at work in people's lives.

When a church or city can't experience revival, perhaps Satan has been doing more homework than Christians have.

For years, I wondered why revival wouldn't take root in Lansing. Every time revival sparked it would be snuffed out. I studied the Bible to see what God's Word says about this situation. I discovered whenever Satan was able to get people's eyes off Jesus and onto issues not essential to salvation, that strife resulted and revival was killed. Knowing that, I work doubly hard to keep my focus, and the focus of the church, on Jesus!

Are you ready to fight and take away spiritual territory from Satan and clean up places the devil has had under his control? Let's get to it!

Where does our authority come from?
Jesus! At Calvary he stripped Satan
of his authority in the earth and
gave it to the Church.

3

AT WAR—LIKE IT OR NOT

I'm fed up with demonic principalities hovering over our cities, holding nets full of unsaved people destined for hell. I'm tired of Christians being blind to the necessity for spiritual warfare against powers in high places. I'm tired of the devil owning more spiritual territory in my city than Christians do.

In his book, *Revivals In Religion*, the great revivalist Charles Finney wrote that a key to having sustained revival is for people to believe the devil has no right to rule this world.

Like it or not, we're at war. What should our response be? Active, full-scale, no-holds-barred, all-out attack!

GETTING READY

What does your spiritual uniform look like? Are you in civilian clothes or fatigues? How does a soldier dress for war?

In 2 Timothy 2:3 we're called soldiers; in Ephesians 6:11 we're told to put on the full armor of God. Part of that armor is the Word of God. In the hands of a believer, God's Word becomes a powerful weapon.

Most Christians fight a defensive war. They passively wait for an attack and then try to ward it off with prayer or fasting. But the Bible says to mount an offensive against the enemy. The Bible gives us a beautiful description of the weapons of our warfare in 2 Corinthians. We have an active—not a passive—role to play.

> **For though we walk in the flesh, we do not war after the flesh:**
> **(For the weapons of our warfare are not carnal, but mighty through God to the pulling down of strong holds;)**
> **Casting down imaginations, and every high thing that exalteth itself against the knowledge of God, and bringing into captivity every thought to the obedience of Christ;**
> **—2 Corinthians 10:3–5**

Our weapons are not the weapons of the world. On the contrary, they have divine power to demolish strongholds.

Demolishing is an active thing to do. One of the reasons America lost the war in Vietnam was because our soldiers weren't allowed to launch offensives against the enemy. We had to wait for our enemies to attack and then try to fight them off. I was in that combat zone for thirteen months, and the only thing we could do was lay down "harassing" fire. We weren't allowed to cross certain lines, and that policy cost America the war.

Christians fight their own Vietnam everyday. They pray a little, which is like harassing fire, but—too often—they don't launch an offensive against the enemy.

I don't believe Satan has the right to open an "adult" bookstore in my city. He tried to do it a few blocks from the church, and we started calling forth God's will for that piece of property before that bookstore ever got rooted. In about a month, that store was bankrupt and gone! A print shop moved in and became our church's printer.

We need to take an aggressive stand against the enemy, not passively sit back!

WHO'S IN CHARGE?

Imagine an army where the soldiers wander around not knowing who's giving the orders. Christian believers can be that way. They suffer and are harassed, not realizing they've been given the authority and power to win the war.

Where does our authority come from? Jesus! At Calvary he stripped Satan of his authority in the earth and gave it to the Church. He said:

> Behold, I give unto you power to tread on serpents and scorpions, and over all the power of the enemy: and nothing shall by any means hurt you.
> —Luke 10:19

Jesus handed us the opportunity to get experience in spiritual warfare on earth so that someday we can be co-rulers with him!

During the days of the Roman Empire, when a Roman general made a great conquest, all the enemy soldiers were stripped of their armor and tied to the back of Roman chariots and paraded through the town. The conqueror made an open show of the enemy so that everyone would know they were now powerless.

Between the time he died on the cross and rose from the dead, Jesus went to hell, stripped Satan of his power and took away all his authority. The devil was forever broken. Like a Roman conqueror, Jesus made an open show of Satan. He paraded the broken powers of darkness throughout the regions of hell!

> Beware lest any man spoil you through philosophy and vain deceit, after the tradition of men, after the rudiments of the world, and not after Christ.

35

> For in him dwelleth all the fulness of the Godhead bodily.
>
> And ye are complete in him, which is the head of all principality and power:
>
> In whom also ye are circumcised with the circumcision made without hands, in putting off the body of the sins of the flesh by the circumcision of Christ:
>
> Buried with him in baptism, wherein also ye are risen with him through the faith of the operation of God, who hath raised him from the dead.
>
> And you, being dead in your sins and the uncircumcision of your flesh, hath he quickened together with him, having forgiven you all trespasses;
>
> Blotting out the handwriting of ordinances that was against us, which was contrary to us, and took it out of the way, nailing it to his cross;
>
> And having spoiled principalities and powers, he made a shew of them openly, triumphing over them in it.
>
> —Colossians 2:8–15

We must clearly understand the devil doesn't have any right to walk all over us. He doesn't have any right to tell the Church of Jesus Christ what to do. Right now, Satan is operating illegally. The only power he has comes by tricking us into giving him some of our power. You wouldn't let your neighbor run a power cord from your house to light his house but, spiritually speaking, that's what the devil does.

Jesus said:

> And I will give you the keys of the Kingdom of Heaven. Whatever you forbid on earth will be forbidden in heaven, and whatever you permit on earth will be permitted in heaven."
>
> —Matthew 16:19 (NLT)

He emphatically proclaimed the gates of hell would never prevail against the Church (Matthew 16:18). Hell can only prevail against those who haven't claimed Jesus' authority for their lives.

We, as believers, are his representatives to do the same works he did, and even greater works. When he was a man, Jesus could only be in one place at a time; now his divine presence is spread throughout the world! So when we are in accord with him, and the Holy Spirit lives in us, we can accomplish anything.

When God's people are on the move, the enemy is very afraid. In Numbers 22:1 we read that the children of Israel traveled to the plains of Moab and camped there. Moab and the Amorites were sworn enemies of Israel.

> **And when the people of Moab saw how many**
> **Israelites there were, they were terrified.**
> **—Numbers 22:3 (NLT)**

We want the devil to be distressed because of us just like Israel's enemy was distressed because of them. Our enemy trembles because he knows the power we have—if we use it.

Are you using your power, or letting the devil walk all over you? Are you bound or free?

Now is the time to realize that the devil has no legal authority to mess up your life.

4

HOW SATAN BINDS PEOPLE

Once a woman came to my Bible study class. As she was leaving she said, "Pray for me. That dirty devil is making me smoke cigarettes and drink and go to dances and card parties."

I replied, "The dirty devil isn't making you do any of those things, it's the dirty ole' you!"

If Satan binds a person, he or she is bound for one of two reasons: either by the active choice of that person to willfully and intentionally sin, or the person doesn't know that Jesus came to set the sinner free and he accomplished that on Calvary. The devil has no power to make you go to card parties and dances or to smoke or drink. He has no legal right on this earth to make you do anything. You sin by your own choice or through ignorance—that's all there is to it.

One woman called me and said, "Could you tell me why I drink?" I said, "Yes, because you want to." She said, "But I want the Lord so bad." However, she also wanted to drink. She was bound by choice.

James 4:7 instructs us to resist the devil and he will flee. The only view of the devil Christians should see is his backside running away!

IT'S YOUR CHOICE

In Acts, Paul explained that God sent him to the Gentiles:

> To open their eyes, and to turn them from
> darkness to light, and from the power of Satan
> unto God....
>
> —Acts 26:18a

A person who has not received forgiveness from Jesus Christ will be influenced by the powers of Satan. This is confirmed in Ephesians:

> And you hath he quickened, who were dead in
> trespasses and sins;
> Wherein in time past ye walked according to
> the course of this world, according to the prince of
> the power of the air, the spirit that now worketh in
> the children of disobedience.
>
> — Ephesians 2:1–2

First John 3:8a says:

> He that committeth sin is of the devil; for the
> devil sinneth from the beginning....

"He that committeth sin" in the Greek actually means he that makes a continual practice of sin, caring less about the will of God. John continues:

> For this purpose the Son of God was manifest-
> ed, that he might destroy the works of the devil.
>
> —1 John 3:8b

The word "destroy" means to break or undo. The devil tied everybody up in knots of sin, knots of sickness, and knots of oppression. Jesus came and undid the knots Satan tied around the human race.

If you are a "born-again" Christian, you have been re-leased from the bondage of the works of the devil! Sin can no longer grip you, unless you allow it.

CASTING OUT THE ENEMY

The devil wants to trick you and lure you away from God's purpose. For instance, someone perceives a "fault" in their pastor, or gets offended by someone in the church, and leaves. The devil has now successfully led them astray—away from where God planted them. The devil should not be pulling your strings; you should be casting him out of every situation. Remember, Jesus said:

> **And these signs shall follow them that believe;**
> **In my name shall they cast out devils; they shall**
> **speak with new tongues....**
> —Mark 16:17

No one should be led astray or bound by sin. To say that Jesus didn't completely disarm Satan is to say that Jesus failed in his mission. No! Jesus did not fail, and it's time for us to take authority over the devil and not let him bind up our kids, families, jobs, churches, or any other aspect of our lives.

AN EXAMPLE OF SEIZING VICTORY

A "divine" meditation center opened in my neighbor-hood, so everyday I made a point to walk by and say, "In the Name of Jesus, I command this place to go out of business. I bind the forces of darkness behind it." I announced to people that it would soon be out of business. One day I went by and the sign was down. I was jubilant—and I quit praying about it. A few days later, a new sign was up: "Divine Meditation Library." I started to pray again, and after a few weeks that place closed down and a good business moved in.

We must take an aggressive stand against the enemy and tell him to get his hands off our street corners. We're soldiers of Jesus Christ, we share in his authority according to the Word. It is imperative that we use that authority!

Alice was a maid in a big hotel in Oklahoma City where evangelists would stay when they held crusades. Alice loved cleaning their rooms and would praise the Lord as she cheerfully went about her work. One day she came in to work with a sad face. A visiting evangelist asked what was wrong. She said, "I've let the devil take right over. He's got control of me now." She showed him a letter from a ministry that read:

> *"Dear Alice, for the last three months you have failed to send in your pledge. Therefore, we are removing the presence of God from your house, and we are loosing a curse upon you."*

The evangelist saw through the ploy and told Alice she had authority in Christ that no one could take away. They began to pray and she started jumping up and down saying, "I've got authority over the devil!" She ran home and started claiming authority in the Name of Jesus over her house and over her unsaved husband. It wasn't long before he broke down and gave his heart to the Lord. The satanic influence over her life was broken when Alice realized the devil's authority was illegal.

Maybe you feel like your life is in a mess. Perhaps it seems like the devil has been attacking you on all fronts. You've seen him at work in your family, your financial situation, and your business. Now is the time to realize that the devil has no legal authority to mess up your life.

If the Son therefore shall make you free, ye shall be free indeed.

—John 8:36

Now, let's look at the three main levels of spiritual warfare.

It's exciting to know that after trying every worldly solution, you can receive the answer to the problem by using the power Jesus gave us all at Calvary!

5

LEVELS OF DEMONS

There are three levels of spiritual warfare:

1. **Ground-level warfare.**
2. **Second-level warfare.**
3. **Strategic-level warfare.**

EVERY DAY DEVILS

I learned about ground-level warfare when I first became a pastor. Up to that point, I knew a lot of Scripture verses about casting out demons, but I didn't grasp the reality of it. I certainly found out fast.

One week after I became pastor, I received a telephone call from a member of my church saying, "Pastor, could you come over? There's something strange going on with our daughter-in-law. She's acting like a mountain lion." I arrived to see a woman in a leopard-skin outfit lying on the floor curling her fingers into claws and hissing. She looked at me and in a demonic-sounding voice said, "I ha-a-a-te yo-ou-ou."

I knew the Bible verse about casting out demons was going to be put to the test right then! I asked her, "What's wrong with you?" She replied, "You're what's wrong with me." She kept spitting and snarling and hissing. However, I was not dismayed; peace flooded my soul, and I took that as a sign from God that the demon would be cast out.

I leaned over her, put my hands on her head and said, "In the Name of Jesus Christ, come out of her!" She shook violently. I repeated, "Come out of her in the Name of Jesus!" Suddenly, she went limp. Her eyes opened; she lifted her head and said, "What happened?" I answered, "A demon just left. What did you do to draw that demon into your life?" She started crying and said she'd been using illegal drugs. By doing so, she had built a stronghold in her life and the enemy moved right in.

A DEMON?

Once I received a call from one of our deacons who said something serious was happening to his wife. I arrived to find her in bed trying to rip her clothes off. She looked at me and said, "I'm Lucifer, and I'm going to kill her." I said, "In the name of Jesus, no you are not!" I rebuked the demon for around two hours, but she didn't get any better. I began to suspect that the devil wasn't causing her problem.

As it turned out, she hadn't slept in five days. We got her to the hospital and, sure enough, the lack of sleep had depleted an important hormone. When they replaced it, she became well.

With years of experience behind me, I've learned to discern demonic activity from other causes of strange behavior. Once, I attended an evangelist's crusade in Detroit. The service started and soon everyone was worshiping, clapping their hands, and praising God—everyone except for one woman dressed in red from head to toe (her face was the only part of her body you could see). She was gyrating around in a very strange way that just "felt" wrong and making strange noises.

The evangelist walked right over to her, put his hands on her head, and said, "In the Name of Jesus, shut up and sit down." That woman went down like a fallen tree.

These are all examples of ground-level warfare. Every believer has the authority to confront demons alone at this first level. Every one of us has family members or friends who are blinded and struggling with demons. It's up to us to break those strongholds in their lives!

Have you ever met someone who says he or she can't quit a certain bad habit? It could be that a demon has built a stronghold. Booting demons out of strongholds is ground-level warfare. It's exciting to know, after trying every worldly solution, you can receive the answer to the problem by using the power Jesus gave you at Calvary. You can't always get results from self-help books, social programs, political action, counseling, a doctor's prescription, or throwing money at the problem. However, in many cases ground-level warfare works.

SECOND-LEVEL WARFARE

The second level of spiritual warfare places you in conflict against powers of a higher order than run-of-the-mill demons. They work through shamans, witches, satanists, New Age "channelers," and occultists. They seem to be a bit stronger than first-level demons.

Common demons go at your command. There has been confusion why some demons come out in two minutes and others take hours. Some Christians conclude they don't have the spiritual power to successfully wage war against them, but different demons have different strengths. It takes discernment, spiritual maturity, and experience to recognize your foe.

I was sitting in a restaurant one evening when a man came over and said,

"I really need to tell you something. I was born in Mexico, and when I lived there I practiced voodoo. When I got to the United States, I heard your church invested heavily in missions to Mexico. People in my religion hate that because the missionaries always seem to destroy our religion. One Saturday I came over to your church and positioned myself on the berm, and all day long I put curses and hexes on your church. I prayed to my gods that your church would burn down.

"After dusk, I felt a release that the job was done; the curse was there, and I could go home. When I went home, there were fire engines on my street. My house had burned to the ground! I realized then that your God was more powerful than mine. I came to church the next Sunday morning to find out about your God, and when you gave the invitation to accept Jesus, I was the first one to go down and receive him as my Savior!"

Even though he was working with demons at this second level, his curse got reversed! The Bible says, "...the curse causeless shall not come" (Proverbs 26:2).

I believe if our church wasn't a praying church, we could have been harmed. We have prayer meetings every morning, revival rallies, a committed team of regular intercessors, and many other prayer opportunities. We unite in prayer often. That's what it takes to repel and reverse the work of second-level demons. A few people united in prayer make all the difference.

STRATEGIC-LEVEL WARFARE

Then there is strategic-level warfare. I knew nothing about this type of warfare for years. When you're dealing with ground-level warfare, you can handle it alone if you stay prayed up. When you're dealing with second-level warfare, get a couple of people to pray with you. When you're dealing with strategic-level warfare, get a crowd. These powerful demons control cities and work on a large scale.

A group of Christian kids heard a satanic rock band was coming to Traverse City, Michigan, so the kids got together and started praying that God would thwart their plans. On the night of the concert, the band was set up and ready to go, and the Christians wondered if their prayers would go unanswered.

The announcer introduced the band, and as they came out their equipment blew up. The concert never happened!

Later, I will describe in greater detail strategic-level demons in Satan's army. But first, how do you know when the devil is at work? Let's look at the character of this hideous being so you can recognize his "fingerprints" in any situation—and give him the boot.

*Satan lies about anything and everything.
These days we especially find him
attacking the fundamental
truths of our faith and
casting doubt upon
the Word of God.*

6

CHARACTERISTICS OF SATAN

During World War II, American sailors studied outlines of enemy ships. They knew the silhouettes of every enemy ship and could tell at a glance, day or night, if an approaching ship was friend or foe. Quick identification of the enemy meant they could fire first and win the battle.

The same principle is true in spiritual warfare. If you can identify the enemy, you've solved half the problem. So what are Satan's characteristics? What does his silhouette look like against the horizon? How can you spot him with a glance, day or night?

Jesus, our supreme commander, lists a few characteristics of the enemy in the Bible.

> **He was a murderer from the beginning, and abode not in the truth, because there is no truth in him. When he speaketh a lie, he speaketh of his own: for he is a liar, and the father of it.**
> **—John 8:44b**

Satan's nature is to lie. He tells white lies, black lies, red lies, purple lies. He stretches the truth, exaggerates, misleads, and traffics in dishonesty. Jesus said the truth sets people free

(John 8:32). Here we are told that in Satan there is no truth, so he cannot set people free. The only thing he can do is trap, trick, and bind people with deception and misery.

It first happened in the Garden of Eden. Satan told Adam and Eve, "You shall not die," when God had told them, "If you eat of this fruit you will die." The first words from Satan's mouth were lies (see Genesis 3).

LYING TO A PREACHER

The late C.M. Ward, the great *Revival Time* radio host and preacher of years past, told a story about his early ministry when Satan lied to him. Ward's ministry was off to a good start, but he had a morbid fear of dying of a heart attack at an early age. He held on to that lie, and fear began to grip him. He worried constantly that his heart would stop at any minute; his imagination made him a nervous wreck. He couldn't preach properly. He was hamstrung by fear.

Then he made a commitment to another church to fill the pulpit while the regular pastor was on vacation. As he stood before this congregation, he felt like an empty shell. Suddenly, an elderly woman, a housewife, stood up and said, "Brother Ward, I recognize that you're oppressed by Satan. There is a spiritual battle going on in your life, and he's using worry to ruin your health. Satan put that thought in your mind." Ward stood there flabbergasted.

The woman walked up on the platform, laid her motherly hands on his head and commanded, "Satan, in the Name of Jesus Christ get your hands off Brother Ward! Brother Ward, in the Name of Jesus, be free of this condition!"

From that moment, he was completely delivered from the bondage of fear. He went on to become a great evangelist and a towering figure in the Assemblies of God movement.

FEAR HITS HOME

I, too, was gripped by fear of a heart attack for many years. One morning, I was praying in the sanctuary in the early hours when a crushing pain stabbed through my chest. It felt like my whole chest was caving in. My left arm numbed, and I panted for air. I thought, "Your dad died of heart problems at a very young age; your grandpa died of heart problems at a very young age. It's probably your time to go. God is calling you home." Then the thought came to me, "Wouldn't that be my luck? I just became pastor at Mount Hope Church and here I go."

Then I recognized who was telling me those lies, and I said, "Devil, in the Name of Jesus take your hands off me. I can't die right now; God's called me to do a work in Lansing and it's not done yet. Get your hands off me in the Name of Jesus." It worked! I took off like a bolt of lightning and ran around the church and within minutes the pain and numbness were gone.

DECEIVING DOCTRINE

Satan lies about anything and everything. These days we especially find him attacking the fundamental truths of our faith and casting doubt upon the Word of God. "Is it really infallible?" "Did God really inspire the Bible?" "The Bible is a 'fluid' document and its meaning changes with the times. It is not absolute." Satan busily spins his web of lies.

He casts doubt on the deity of Jesus and tries to make people believe Christ was nothing more than an angel, or a "good" man who worked his way up to becoming a "god." The devil attacks divine healing and says it passed away with the Apostles. He says that the gifts of the Spirit are not needed anymore because now we have better education. He says salvation is not by faith but by knocking on so many doors.

Satan is a dishonest broker. He's worse than the worst shifty, corrupt salesman you've ever encountered. He's bold in his lies.

What makes a person susceptible to the devil's web of lies? Let's take a look at some potential areas of weakness that Satan can use against you to create problems in your life.

An absence of truth creates a vacuum,
that draws in lies like a vacuum
cleaner draws in dirt.

7

WHY PEOPLE FALL FOR LIES

What opens a person up to satanic lies? There are three main conditions: a vacuum or absence of truth, idleness or an unguarded mind, and taking your eyes off Jesus.

A VACUUM OR ABSENCE OF TRUTH

If you don't plant good seeds in an empty field, weeds soon spring up. The bad seeds drift in on the air, or birds and animals bring them. The next thing you know you have a field full of thriving, useless weeds.

Our minds are like empty fields. If we don't plant truth, they become wide open for lies. Nothing can exist in a vacuum. Something always rushes in to fill it. An absence of truth creates a vacuum that draws in lies like a vacuum cleaner draws in dirt.

> **Jesus said to the people who believed in him, "You are truly my disciples if you remain faithful to my teachings.**
> **And you will know the truth, and the truth will set you free."**
> **—John 8:31–32 (NLT)**

Do you want to walk in freedom from lies? Fill your mind and heart with God's Word. His healthy "seeds" will muscle out any weed seeds that blow in.

ONE WAY BAD SEEDS ARE PLANTED

Before I knew the Word of God, I used to listen to lots of secular music. Recently I was going through some of my old records and was surprised to see how I had once programmed myself with lies through music. One song, *The Last Kiss* by J. Frank Wilson and the Cavaliers has a chorus that says,

> *"Where oh where can my baby be?*
> *The Lord took her away from me.*
> *She's gone to Heaven so I've got to be good,*
> *So I can see my baby when I leave this world."*

The song tells how God supposedly caused an accident that killed his girlfriend. In that one lyric are two pieces of false doctrine. First, God doesn't cause accidents. Second, you don't go to Heaven by being good. You go to Heaven by believing in Jesus Christ and receiving him as your Savior by faith. Yet that song probably defined my theology for many years!

Then there was *Daddy, What is Heaven Like?* by Tiny Tim:

> *" 'Daddy, Daddy, what is heaven like?*
> *Is it like our house, so pretty and white?*
> *I don't understand, it doesn't seem fair.*
> *If Mommy loved us so, why did she go there?'*

> *" 'Heaven, my son is a beautiful place.*
> *Where there's a smile on everyone's face.*
> *Mommy loved us both, but she had to go,*
> *We needed her so, but they needed her more....'*

" 'And maybe someday, you'll go to heaven, too.
If I know your mommy, she saved a place for you.' "

Once again there is "weedy" thinking in these lyrics. First, God doesn't kill mothers. Second, you don't get to Heaven because someone saves you a place.

Norman Greenbaum had a hit song *Spirit in the Sky* which says,

> *"Never been a sinner I never sinned,*
> *I got a friend in Jesus,*
> *So you know that when I die,*
> *He's gonna set me up with,*
> *The spirit in the sky."*

It was a popular song when I was growing up, but the Bible says *all* have sinned and fallen short of the glory of God (Romans 3:23). The man in this song claimed he never sinned, and that would be impossible.

After awhile I quit studying those old lyrics because there were literally hundreds of songs that contained false ideas. I had let their lyrics into my mind where they insidiously influenced my thinking. It was depressing just to consider it. Now, I know better! Now I plant truth where those "weeds" once grew.

IDLENESS OR AN UNGUARDED MIND

My friend Jim served in Vietnam and liked to write music. He wasn't a Christian. While he was overseas, Jim's "friends" told him cocaine and opium-laced marijuana would make him more creative in his composing. He took their advice, and his music got more base and lewd and had the smell of hell's smoke on it. He took hallucinogenic drugs, ended up in a coma, and they put him in an asylum in Florida. Jim hadn't guarded his mind. He let lies sneak into it through an open gate created by drugs and they devoured him.

However, his Uncle Jack visited him every day. His uncle realized Satan was trying to kill Jim. The doctor said Jim would remain comatose—a vegetable—but Jack read the Bible and spoke words of God's truth into Jim's ears as he lay unconscious in his bed.

He'd say, "Jim, you have believed the lies of the devil. It brought you into bondage. Now believe the truth of Jesus and become free." One day Jim opened his eyes, and the doctors were astonished. He ultimately regained consciousness and accepted Jesus Christ as his Lord. The truth saved Jim, his brain healed, and he's ministering the Gospel today.

TAKING YOUR EYES OFF JESUS

The only safe place for your eyes to linger is on Jesus. If you stare at people long enough you'll become disillusioned and find yourself open to satanic lies. Jesus' plans and ideas are not of this world. They are life and truth, and they'll never let you down. Make Jesus the focus of your life and your eyes won't stray where they don't belong. Also, you will begin to recognize Satan at work.

People get confused and think God causes sickness—but that's not true.

8

EXPOSING SATAN'S WORKS

What are the works of the devil? What does he do? What does he make happen on the earth?

SIN

The first work of the devil is sin. He was the original sinner. There is no record of any creature sinning before him.

He promotes sin and reminds you of sin. If he can't get you to sin in the present moment, he'll remind you of past sins—despite the fact that Jesus destroyed the power of guilt from past sins. Satan wants you to live in a hall of mirrors where anywhere you look you see your sin reflected back at you.

SICKNESS

Sin destroys your spirit, but the devil also wants to destroy your physical body. That's why his second work is sickness. People get confused and think God causes sickness—but that's not true. In Job 2:7 it was the devil that afflicted Job with boils. In Luke 13, Satan had bound a woman with a spirit of infirmity that caused her to be bent over; she could not straighten up. Sickness is a work of the devil. Does that mean that everybody who gets sick is demon possessed? No! But the nature of sickness comes from the devil.

If we think that sickness comes from God, how could we possibly pray a prayer of faith for healing? How can you pray to a God who causes sickness? No, Jesus healed all that were oppressed of the devil. He removed sickness!

> **How God anointed Jesus of Nazareth with the Holy Ghost and with power: who went about doing good, and healing all that were oppressed of the devil; for God was with him.**
>
> **—Acts 10:38**

Peter's mother-in-law had a fever (see Luke 4:39). There is no record that she was possessed by a demon, but Jesus rebuked the sickness and it left. That tells us the basic nature of the fever.

Smith Wigglesworth, the great apostle of faith, suffered from appendicitis and couldn't seem to get healed. Thousands had been healed in his ministry, but he couldn't get healed himself. An elderly Christian woman came into the room where he lay, looked at his stomach, and slugged him in his side saying, "In the Name of Jesus you come out of there," and Wigglesworth was healed. God had given her discernment into the spirit world, and she saw a demon with its hands on Wigglesworth's appendix.

How do you feel when someone you love is sick? You want to help! That's how God feels when we're sick. I've heard dozens of stories and had many firsthand experiences of people successfully rebuking the devil's attack through sickness.

Maybe you're oppressed of the devil today. Jesus is the same today as he was back then! He doesn't want you sick. You can stand up to that sickness and rebuke the devil just like Jesus and the apostles did. Don't let Satan get his grip on your physical health.

STORMS

The third major work of the devil is destructive storms. Insurance companies call floods, tornadoes, lightning, and hurricanes "acts" of God, but the Bible says they're the devil's work. In Job 1:18–20 the devil brought a destructive storm to Job's house. In Mark 4:35–41 the disciples were crossing the sea with Jesus when a tremendous storm came up, and Jesus rebuked it. If that storm were an act of God, would Jesus be able to rebuke it? Wouldn't that be dividing a kingdom against itself?

Just like sickness and sin, storms can be combated. Don Hughes had a house in Broken Arrow, Oklahoma. He was home with his family one night when the weather service issued a tornado warning. Don walked around his property praying, "Father, in Jesus' Name, you gave me this property. You said angels are ministering spirits. I pray that you will put angels on the corners of this property. No storm is going to come near this dwelling. I claim protection for my property, my family, and our lives."

He walked onto the porch and felt an eerie heaviness in the air. The skies darkened; he saw an ominous black cloud in the southwest. It became a funnel cloud, and he heard the terrifying roaring sound of rushing wind. The funnel cloud was coming right toward his neighborhood.

He sat down in the living room praising God for his protection. The funnel cloud drew closer and closer. But when it got to his neighborhood, suddenly it lifted like a helicopter and was never seen again. His house was undamaged!

Jesus has given Christians authority over storms!

PRAY AGAINST THE STORM

One woman in Texas wasn't sure about claiming protection for her property, but she claimed protection for her life during a tornado. She cried out, "Jesus," as her home lifted off its foundation and blew away. She stayed right there without a hair on her head out of place. God protected her.

A well-known evangelist was setting up $145,000 worth of musical equipment in a stadium for a crusade (a grand piano and microphone systems), but weathermen were predicting a serious storm that could cause flash flooding. Revival hadn't hit this town in a long time. The seeds had been planted, so instead of calling the rally off they set up their equipment as big black clouds hovered overhead. They commanded in faith, "In the Name of Jesus, storm you hold off because we're having revival here tonight."

People started coming. The bleachers filled. That day more people came to know Jesus than the evangelist had ever seen before in his crusades.

After the last person left, the crew repacked the equipment. As they latched the last semi-truck door, the rain broke loose. The storm had gone right up to the stadium, took the shape of a banana and went around it. Not a drop of rain fell inside. You may think it a coincidence, but I say Christians have more authority over the actions of the devil than you might think.

IT WORKS!

I even have my own example. One time, I let somebody talk me into insulating my attic. I'm anything but handy; I usually come out of home improvement projects black and blue. However, I was convinced we would save money on the heating bill if we insulated. I had one day off, and weather reports said there was a 100 percent chance of rain. My wife, Mary Jo, and I picked up the insulation machine and drove to our house to do this job that someone else should have been doing. Raindrops started hitting the windshield and we prayed, "Lord, we've only got one day to do this. Please hold off the rain." I looked up to the clouds and I said, "In the Name of Jesus, hold off until we're done."

All of a sudden it quit—no more raindrops. We got home, and Mary Jo got to work cutting the bags open and dumping them into this big machine. I was sweating in the oppressively hot attic shooting the stuff around and thanking God for holding off the rain because when insulation gets wet it's a terrible mess. We finally got the job done. Somehow insulation also ended up in the living room—and even in the basement—but we finished. We got the machine back on the truck and I looked up at the sky and said, "Okay, let 'er loose," and at that instant—crack—thunder rolled, lightning flashed, and it rained!

That may seem coincidental to you, but to me it was a miracle. Destructive storms and weather disturbances are works of the devil. Jesus has already undone Satan's work. So, I'm going to take Jesus' victory and Jesus' authority, and I'm going to do anything I can to thwart the devil's plans!

Spiritual blindness must be combated spiritually. True evangelism is never accomplished through human persuasion.

9

SPIRITUAL BLINDNESS AND FALSE RELIGIONS

Some other works of the devil are spiritual blindness and false religions.

> If the Good News we preach is hidden behind a veil, it is hidden only from people who are perishing.
> Satan, who is the god of this world, has blinded the minds of those who don't believe. They are unable to see the glorious light of the Good News. They don't understand this message about the glory of Christ, who is the exact likeness of God
> —2 Corinthians 4:3–4 (NLT)

Have you ever talked to somebody about your Christian faith, pouring your heart out, and they still could not see it? It's like a solid wall goes up between you and them, and they simply can't "hear" what you're saying. The likely cause is spiritual blindness.

I spoke with a man who was involved with one of today's more aggressive cults. He didn't believe that Jesus was actually God. I showed him Bible verse after Bible verse, but he would only argue and fight with me. One day, he got so mad at me he began cussing and accusing me of being demon possessed. I was so frustrated I wanted to pull my hair out. Then the answer came to my spirit. Satan, the god of this world, had shut his mind to the truth. He was like a blind man, totally unable to see.

WHEN BLINDNESS FALLS

Some of the blindest people in the Bible were the Pharisees, whom Jesus called blind guides. It wasn't that they would not believe, they simply could not believe. Why? Because the god of this world had blinded their "spiritual" eyes and they could not see the truth.

This blindness spread to the people. Can you imagine the crowd yelling, "Crucify him!"? Jesus had healed and taught them for over three years, and suddenly they turned on him with cries of, "Send him to the cross!" The Bible said that if they had known, they would never have had Jesus crucified (1 Corinthians 2:8). Blindness came over them.

Spiritual blindness must be combated spiritually. True evangelism is never accomplished through human persuasion. It's a divine work that begins with opening the spiritual eyes of the individual so they may "see" the glorious Gospel of Jesus Christ. You can shine a flashlight into a blind man's eyes all you want, but he won't see it unless his eyes work. You can shine the light of truth in people's "spiritual eyes" all you want, but their eyes must be opened before they will believe.

One worldwide evangelist went place-to-place preaching the Gospel, but few people received Christ. The Lord told him he was losing the spiritual battle before services even began. The people's minds were closed. He changed his methods, and before service he prayed that spiritual blindness would be broken and that scales would fall off people's eyes. In the very first service after he prayed this way, hundreds of people received Christ!

A well-known pastor in Memphis, Tennessee, would see people saved in every service. He was asked what his "secret" was, and he replied, "It's in the prayer room that the battles are won or lost." He had learned the secret that true evangelism doesn't take place by human persuasion. It takes place in the spirit.

On the day of Pentecost, when Peter preached his great message, three thousand people were saved. Did this happen because Peter was such a good preacher? No. Was it because he was filled with the Holy Spirit? Well, that helped. But the main reason was because Peter and his team had spent ten days in praise, prayer, and worship of God. Therefore, the Bible says the Holy Spirit pricked the hearts and minds of the people who had been blinded by Satan so they could see the truth (Acts 2:37). By the time Peter preached the Good News, their blindness had already been lifted!

WRONG-HEADED RELIGIONS

Some religions preach Jesus—but it's a false Jesus. There are huge, well-organized churches based on lies or false representations of God. This is a work of the devil, and it seems to have accelerated in these last days.

> And as he sat upon the mount of Olives, the disciples came unto him privately, saying, Tell us, when shall these things be? And what shall be the sign of thy coming, and of the end of the world?
>
> And Jesus answered and said unto them, Take heed that no man deceive you.
>
> For many shall come in my name, saying, I am Christ; and shall deceive many.
>
> And many false prophets shall rise, and shall deceive many.
>
> — Matthew 24:3–5 & 11

Have you ever spoken with a member of a false religion? Sometimes they're normal, kind people. Sometimes they're aggressive in wanting to convert you. But anyone who believes a Gospel different than the one presented in the Bible, has fallen into a trap of the devil. False religious systems actually have seducing spirits, which propagate teachings that originate in the pits of hell.

> **Now the Spirit speaketh expressly, that in the latter times some shall depart from the faith, giving heed to seducing spirits, and doctrines of devils.**
> **—1 Timothy 4:1**

Satan is the mastermind of every false religion. A false apostle or prophet or teacher may claim to have a special message from God, but they really don't. They may claim to be sent by God, but they're really not. The rise of cults today is a clear indication that we are nearing the return of Jesus Christ.

Here are five ways to recognize false prophets and combat false religions and cults.

1. They may claim that all religious bodies are apostate—except for their own.

There is an "exclusive" aura around false religions. They claim to have deeper truths than anybody else. They want to control you, and they don't want you listening to anyone else. They say, "Only listen to our teaching. Only read our books. We are God's faithful remnant on the earth."

2. They focus on minor issues rather than on Jesus Christ.

The last thing the devil wants is to give Jesus any airtime, so his false ministers focus on minor doctrinal points, pulling passages out of context so they become distorted. Even truth can become untruth if it's taken out of context.

3. They place undue emphasis on the written works of non-biblical authors.

It's not wrong to read books, but no book is equal to Scripture. Any group that says their special book is a source of infallible truth is operating under a seducing spirit. No book in the world is to be taken as equivalent to the Scriptures. One famous cult leader who has a university named for him said, "I have never written anything in my life that cannot be taken on an equal par as the Scriptures." When you hear things like that, you know that you are hearing a false prophet.

4. They teach non-biblical things about Jesus Christ.

Jesus Christ is the central person in the Bible from Genesis to Revelation. He is the eternal Son of God. Anyone who denies Jesus is God, was born of a virgin, became a man, lived a sinless life, died on a cross, was bodily resurrected, and will return again is a false prophet. St. John warned that anyone who denies the doctrine of Christ is motivated by the spirit of Antichrist.

5. They promote salvation by means other than individual repentance and faith in Jesus Christ.

Some false religions make followers sell flowers or peanuts or knock on doors as a prerequisite to salvation. They are works-oriented, not grace-oriented. The good news of the Gospel is that we can never earn the grace we need—but God gives it freely through Jesus Christ! You can't put a price tag on it, but false religions try.

What do we do about all this? The only answer to false religion is the true message of Christ. Yes it sounds simple, but it's the solution that turns occult "isms" into occult "wasims."

One missionary held a large crusade in a foreign nation. Thousands attended, but false teachers tried to keep people away. The missionary issued a challenge: "Gather one hundred deaf people and bring them here. You pray in the name of your god, and I'll pray in the name of my God. Whichever God heals them is the living God."

It wasn't hard to find 100 deaf people in a crowd of tens of thousands. They lined up. The false leaders came along and did their hokey pokey and cried out to their god and nothing happened. Then the missionary laid hands on them one by one and said, "In the Name of Jesus Christ, be healed." Ninety-nine were healed of deafness.

When we preach the true Gospel, it comes with power!

Phillip, one of the original deacons, went to Samaria and preached the simple message of Christ. Demons were expelled, miracles were wrought, and there was great joy in that city. Also in that city there was a man named Simon the Sorcerer, an occult leader. When he heard the Gospel and saw its power, he wanted to become a follower of the true God (see Acts 8:13).

Elymas was an occult leader who caused mischief for Paul until the apostle cursed him. A mist came over Elymas' eyes and he was blind (Acts 13:6-12).

In Acts 19:19 people burned a fortune's worth of sorcery books and artifacts when they received the glorious Gospel of Jesus.

You and I can overcome the work of the devil if we pray and preach the full Gospel of Jesus. False religions can't stand up to the spiritual reality of the one and only true Gospel. Turn those "isms" into "wasims."

The next section of this book is critical to understanding the devil's battle plan. It talks about one of his leading generals—a devilish creature with a devilish name.

SECTION TWO

BELIAL

*There are spiritual territories throughout
the world, and each city, neighborhood,
or home can have one of two rulers—
Jesus or the devil.*

10

A SINISTER GENERAL

Have you ever driven into a city or neighborhood and felt uneasy or anxious? Or, have you walked into a restaurant or business and felt on edge for some unknown reason? Were those feelings just random? No, those feelings probably reflect spiritual sensitivity.

Some places feel great—some feel terrible—depending on who is in charge spiritually. There are spiritual territories throughout the world, and each city, neighborhood, or home can have one of two rulers—Jesus or the devil. Satan tries to set up territorial demons over cities, regions, cultures, and individuals to keep them in bondage and under his domination.

While the purpose of this book is not to introduce an exhaustive list of satanic personalities, I want to identify a few of Satan's top generals.

Hebrew scholars believed, and taught, that there were actual spiritual personalities behind names such as "Mammon" and "Belial."

- **Mammon**
  Today we have a tendency to relegate mammon to mere money, yet the Hebrews understood that behind the sins of greed, covetousness, and stinginess was an actual satanic being named Mammon. The same is true of other names of

powerful demonic beings. I deal more in depth with this malignant spirit in my book, *The Road to Radical Riches.*

- **Leviathan**
  This many-headed spirit brings division and discord to churches, families, and businesses. For a deeper study of how this spirit gets a foothold and how to beat him, see my book, *The Miracle Results of Fasting.*

- **Jezebel**
  She was not only a real person, but is the personified demonic spirit operating in witchcraft as Queen Jezebel did. For a comprehensive study on how the Jezebel spirit seeks to control pastors, leaders, and everyone, see my book, *The Jezebel Spirit.* Because this spirit is so prevalent, we will also look at it more deeply later in this book.

- **Belial**
  This was believed to be the strong satanic spirit behind making people's lives worthless. He entices people to do things that bring self-sabotage. Let's take a deeper look at this demonic spirit.

RECOGNIZING BELIAL

Just as we identified the character and works of the devil, we'll look specifically at what this evil henchman of the devil has in store for you and how to stand up to him and send him running.

How do we know Belial is real and not just a myth? In 2 Corinthians Paul says:

> ...for what fellowship hath righteousness with unrighteousness? and what communion hath light with darkness?

> **And what concord hath Christ with Belial?**
> **—2 Corinthians 6:14b–15a**

Belial is mentioned twenty-seven times in the Old Testament, one time in the New Testament, and alluded to many more times than that. Belial appears to be a specific principality, like Leviathan (a crocodile-like spiritual creature), who seeks to tear apart ministries, churches, businesses, and families (Job 41), and Mammon who breeds covetousness, greed, and stealing from God.

Belial's name means without profit, worthless or useless. He lures people into sins that render their lives worthless and barren so nothing they do brings glory to God.

CLING-ONS

Belial has a specific battle plan for your destruction. If he can seduce you into some kind of idolatry, sexual sin, alcohol, or drugs—these are his specialties—then he can attach a demonic "cling-on" to you and bring you under God's judgment.

> **Now the Spirit speaketh expressly, that in the latter times some shall depart from the faith, giving heed to seducing spirits, and doctrines of devils; Speaking lies in hypocrisy; having their conscience seared with a hot iron.**
> **—1 Timothy 4:1–2**

One Bible translation renders the phrase "conscience seared" as "marking them for the devil." This means when you wander too far from the truth, you cause yourself to be marked for destruction.

Does this mean Belial can rob you of your salvation? No. But if he can get you to sin repeatedly in some area, it will create an opening for a demon to cling onto you. A genuine

Christian can not be possessed by the devil, but consistent sinning can build a power base for demons to influence your thoughts and actions. In the end, your life might become complicated and unfruitful—Belial's ultimate goal.

The best way to recognize the work of this sinister character is to study his methods.

A person may play around with
pornography and sexual sin, but soon
there comes a point when their
spirit is corrupted and
they become marked
for destruction.

11

SNARES: IDOLATRY AND SEXUAL SIN

Belial sets up snares to catch the unwitting. He fiercely hunts his prey for destruction. But we can prepare ourselves by studying Belial's strategies as revealed in the Bible. The first two are idolatry and sexual sin.

> **Certain men, the children of Belial, are gone out from among you, and have withdrawn the inhabitants of their city, saying, Let us go and serve other gods, which ye have not known....**
>
> **—Deuteronomy 13:13**

These people were called Belial's "children," meaning they were marked for judgment. How were they seduced? By seeking out other religions.

Christians usually aren't seduced by overt invitations to renounce Christ. Instead, the devil works through people who say, "Let's try transcendental meditation. It's not a religion. You can still be a Christian and practice meditation." Or, "Let's try Scientology. You don't have to give up Jesus." The next thing you know, you're straying from the faith and following another god.

We have many Catholics who worship with us at Mount Hope Church. One Catholic group worshiped Jesus and they saw miracles. But a non-charismatic priest told them, "We're carrying this Jesus thing a little too far. We ought to lift our hands and worship Mary." So they lifted their hands and worshiped Mary, and the miracles stopped.

Recently, I started getting prayer requests from Christian employees of a local hospital. Hospital management allowed the development of a New Age labyrinth and eastern meditation meetings are held there. A woman involved in these practices claims to heal people by magical powers. This same hospital refuses to allow Christians to hold prayer meetings. Belial has successfully seduced these unfortunates into chasing after other gods, thereby marking them for destruction.

False worship can also take the form of unauthorized worship of God—worship that doesn't acknowledge his sovereignty. In the Bible (1 Samuel 2) is the story about the sons of Eli, priests who offered "strange fire" to the Lord. They brought ungodly women into the temple to have sex with them. God called them sons of Belial and marked them for destruction. They died young, never fulfilling the purpose to which they were called.

> Now the sons of Eli were sons of Belial; they knew not the LORD.
>
> And the priest's custom with the people was, that, when any man offered sacrifice, the priest's servant came, while the flesh was in seething, with a fleshhook of three teeth in his hand;
>
> And he struck it into the pan, or kettle, or caldron, or pot; all that the fleshhook brought up the priest took for himself. So they did in Shiloh unto all the Israelites that came thither.
>
> Also before they burnt the fat, the priest's servant came, and said to the man that sacrificed, Give flesh to roast for the priest; for he will not have sodden flesh of thee, but raw.

And if any man said unto him, Let them not
fail to burn the fat presently, and then take as
much as thy soul desireth; then he would answer
him, Nay; but thou shalt give it me now: and if
not, I will take it by force.

Wherefore the sin of the young men was very
great before the LORD: for men abhorred the offering of the LORD....

Now Eli was very old, and heard all that his
sons did unto all Israel; and how they lay with the
women that assembled at the door of the taber-
nacle of the congregation.

And he said unto them, Why do ye such things?
for I hear of your evil dealings by all this people.

Nay, my sons; for it is no good report that I
hear: ye make the LORD's people to transgress.

If one man sin against another, the judge shall
judge him: but if a man sin against the LORD,
who shall intreat for him? Notwithstanding they
hearkened not unto the voice of their father, because the LORD would slay them.

—1 Samuel 2:12–17 & 22–25

The last thing John wrote in his first letter was to "keep
yourselves from idols" (1 John 5:21). My advice is don't take
even a tiny step away from the God of your salvation! Forget
about yoga or eastern meditation and exercise techniques.
Stay away from anything that promotes a spirituality different
from what God has ordained in the Bible.

SEXUAL SINS

The next work of Belial is sexual sin. I knew a minister
whose presence would make me feel like gagging. His presence felt unwholesome. The Lord revealed he had an unclean spirit attached to him, and sure enough he was caught

with a stack of pornographic videos and magazines. He was also caught in adultery.

A person may play around with pornography and sexual sin, but soon there comes a point when their spirit is corrupted and they become marked for destruction. The Bible tells a terrible story:

> Now as they were making their hearts merry, behold, the men of the city, certain sons of Belial, beset the house round about, and beat at the door, and spake to the master of the house, the old man, saying, Bring forth the man that came into thine house, that we may know him.
>
> And the man, the master of the house, went out unto them, and said unto them, Nay, my brethren, nay, I pray you, do not so wickedly; seeing that this man is come into mine house, do not this folly.
>
> Behold, here is my daughter a maiden, and his concubine; them I will bring out now, and humble ye them, and do with them what seemeth good unto you: but unto this man do not so vile a thing.
>
> But the men would not hearken to him: so the man took his concubine, and brought her forth unto them; and they knew her, and abused her all the night until the morning: and when the day began to spring, they let her go.
>
> Then came the woman in the dawning of the day, and fell down at the door of the man's house where her lord was, till it was light.
>
> And her lord rose up in the morning, and opened the doors of the house, and went out to go his way: and, behold, the woman his concubine was fallen down at the door of the house, and her hands were upon the threshold.

> **And he said unto her, up, and let us be going.**
> **But none answered.**
> —Judges 19:22–28a

All sexual sin leads to death. I talked to a doctor who treated a fourteen-year-old girl who was permanently infertile because of venereal disease. Spiritually and physically, sexual sin leaves you barren—and that's exactly what Belial wants.

Belial is behind the acceptance of abortion in America. He deadens our consciences to the fact that abortion is murder.

Belial is behind Internet pornography. A pastor went to a pornographic site by mistake and tried to shut the browser window. But another site popped up, and another, and another. Finally he shut his computer down because he couldn't keep these sites from popping up.

That's the way Belial works. He pops up with seducing enticements. Sometimes, especially for young people, the enticement is a non-Christian boyfriend or girlfriend. A diseased man seduced a young woman in our church. She ended up with HIV. Belial enticed her into a sexual affair that led to her destruction.

Paul says don't "yoke" yourself with unbelievers because it opens the door to demonic influence (2 Corinthians 6:14). I've never seen a successful partnership between a Christian and a non-Christian. But I've seen plenty of young women drawn in by unsaved men thinking they could "change" them. Usually, it brings a curse of strife and division to their home.

If you are a young Christian running around with a non-believing person who's putting on the religious "dog" to attract you, you're looking for trouble! God will never partner with Belial.

These two practices—checking out other gods and dabbling in sexual sin—are Belial's snares. He wants to deaden your conscience, give you a demonic "cling-on," and leave you fruitless.

He utilizes still more snares.

*Belial works to create an atmosphere
of confusion in your life.*

12

SNARES: CONFUSION AND DRUNKENNESS

Belial works to create an atmosphere of confusion in your life. Whenever you deal with him (or any of the devil's generals) situations never make sense. You find yourself in meaningless arguments, strange circumstances, and dead-end conversations without logic or reason.

Years ago, a faithful family attended our church. Everyone loved them. They prayed fervently for their extended family to come to Christ, and one by one they saw it happen. Soon every member of this family was saved. However, as soon as the last person came into the faith, the original family told me they were leaving the church for reasons I still don't understand. They seemed gripped by confusion. Within a few years, two of their children died in strange incidents. They began to develop all kinds of legal problems, and their lives spiraled into confusion. Belial got hold of them and destroyed them.

GRABBING THORNS

Have you ever tried to help someone who is confused? It seems that nothing you say makes a difference. In fact, you often end up getting hurt yourself.

> But the sons of Belial shall be all of them as thorns thrust away, because they cannot be taken with hands:
>
> —2 Samuel 23:6

This verse says dealing with a man with a Belial attachment is like trying to handle thorns without gloves. His business barely muddles along; his family is in constant turmoil. When you try to help him, somehow you end up getting hurt. That's a sign that he is in the Belial's grip.

If you are trying to help someone bound by Belial, there's nothing you can humanly do. Logic, argument, and advice won't work. You must wrestle against the forces of darkness on their behalf to release them from their bondage and confusion.

ALCOHOL

Another weapon in Belial's arsenal is alcohol. In 1 Samuel 1:13–16, the Bible alludes to Belial's seduction of men and women into drunkenness and mind alteration. Hannah was praying, moving her lips without speaking, and the priest thought she was drunk. She protested, "I'm not a daughter of Belial." It was generally understood that Belial and drunkenness were somehow related.

I remember a dinner Mary Jo and I had with a couple from our church. I was shocked when the man—a former board member—poured a glass of wine. He stated, "We believe in having a little wine with our dinner."

I said, "You're kidding me."

He said, "No, it's supposed to aid in digestion and help your heart." Mary Jo and I declined to join him.

In a matter of months this couple's marriage fell apart. I didn't hear from them for years. One day I got a telephone call.

"Pastor Dave."

"Yes?"

"This is Joe (not his real name). I'm at the bar. There's a woman I want you to talk to. I think she really needs the Lord."

It was the former board member, as drunk as could be, acting like a son of Belial. He no longer served God, but he still felt some distant connection, so he became the tavern's resident "evangelist."

He put a woman on the phone and she said, "Joe said I should talk to you because I have this little situation. Mother Mary speaks through me. It happens at the oddest times and I want to be able to control it."

Suddenly, it was like I heard twelve tape recorders going on fast forward all at the same time: ch-ch-ch-ch-ch-ch—a horrible sound! Then this gruff voice said, "I am Mary the mother of God, and you'd better listen to me."

Then the woman spoke in her regular voice, "See, there she is again."

"That came out of you?" I asked.

She replied, "Yes. Mother Mary speaks through me."

I asserted, "Lady, I think you have a demon and need some deliverance."

Then I heard the gruff voice again.

"How dare you say I need deliverance? I'm the mother Mary."

"See, there she is again" I heard her say in a normal voice.

I urged, "Lady, you'd better get over to the church. I'll meet you there with some other pastors, because you need a demon cast out of you!"

Click. The phone went dead. I didn't know what bar they were calling from and never heard from them again.

That's an example of what Belial can do in someone's life through alcohol. Paul wrote:

> Know ye not that the unrighteous shall not inherit the kingdom of God? Be not deceived: neither fornicators, nor idolaters, nor adulterers, nor effeminate, nor abusers of themselves with mankind,
>
> Nor thieves, nor covetous, nor drunkards, nor revilers, nor extortioners, shall inherit the kingdom of God.
>
> —1 Corinthians 6:9–10

Idolatry, sexual sin, confusion, and alcohol abuse are all tools of Belial. But he has even more weapons in his arsenal.

Several Bible passages show us that Belial is behind disrespect of God's appointed men and women in authority.

13

SNARE: DISRESPECTING AUTHORITY

There was a man in our church whose wife was saved, but he was not. He would come to church with his wife, but he never gave money in the offering. He would sneer, "I think that pastor's profiting off the people." I was living in a very poor neighborhood at that time because everything we had went toward building the church. For 14 years my family lived in one of Lansing's poorest neighborhoods while I served the largest church in town. Mary Jo and I gave everything to God. Yet this man said, "I think he's profiting. I think something fishy is going on with the money around here."

Sometimes I wished his wife had never brought him to church! Finally he got the nerve to talk to others about circulating a petition to force the church to publish in the bulletin how much money came in the offering the week before. Of course, it's the members' privilege to know how much money comes in, but not every person off the street is entitled to know the financial affairs of the church.

The very day he proposed his idea, he walked out of the church and suffered a massive heart attack. Was it just coincidence? Or did he align himself with Belial and mark himself for destruction?

TURNED OVER TO SATAN

I've seen people become pawns of Belial by opposing godly men in authority. The symptoms are:

- They accuse or verbally attack God's appointed leaders.
- They treat authority with contempt.
- They make cutting or sarcastic remarks disguised as a joke.

Several Bible passages show us that Belial is behind disrespect of God's appointed men and women in authority. In 1 Samuel, you can read the story of Nabal, a man twice called a son of Belial. David and his men had guarded Nabal's flock all night while he was away shearing his sheep. Then David sent his men to ask for a few supplies:

> **And Nabal answered David's servants, and said, Who is David? and who is the son of Jesse? there be many servants now a days that break away every man from his master.**
> **Shall I then take my bread, and my water, and my flesh that I have killed for my shearers, and give it unto men, whom I know not whence they be?**
> **—1 Samuel 25:10–11**

Nabal was stingy—another sign of a Belial attachment. He returned evil for good. You can never do enough for a person with a Belial attachment. They are never satisfied, and they appreciate nothing.

Even Nabal's own men stood up for David and his men, telling how they had protected the flock, but Nabal still refused to give David provisions. So, David decided to destroy Nabal's family. Do you see how Belial can take down families just by attaching to one person?

But Nabal's wife heard what happened and rode out quickly to intercede with David and bring him supplies.

> Let not my lord, I pray thee, regard this man
> of Belial, even Nabal: for as his name is, so is he;
> Nabal is his name, and folly is with him: but I
> thine handmaid saw not the young men of my
> lord, whom thou didst send.
>
> —1 Samuel 25:25

Again God shows us how intercession is the key to defeating Belial.

Nabal's name meant, "crude, brash, wicked, and worthless." His wife hadn't seen the young men requesting supplies, or she would have given them to David's men.

> And David said to Abigail, Blessed be the
> LORD God of Israel, which sent thee this day to
> meet me:
>
> And blessed be thy advice, and blessed be thou,
> which hast kept me this day from coming to shed
> blood, and from avenging myself with mine own
> hand....
>
> And it came to pass about ten days after, that
> the LORD smote Nabal, that he died.
>
> —1 Samuel 25:32–33, 38

Was it coincidence that Nabal died? No, of course not. You see this pattern demonstrated over and over with people who align themselves with Belial and reject God's anointed men and women.

RESPECTING OUR LEADERS

Once, I had to rebuke a man in my church because he said things about the then-president of the United States. He said, "If he was in front of me right now, I'd kill him. I hate him so much!"

I replied, "Wait a minute. That's overstepping. You may not respect his morals or his character, but God saw fit to make him president of this nation." In Romans 13, the Bible says we're to pray for those in authority, not think about killing them! You want to change somebody's heart when they're in authority? Submit, so far as God's Word permits.

David would not touch the "president" when Saul was king, even though Saul was out to murder him. One night David found Saul sleeping. He had the opportunity to kill him and set himself up as king, and his friends told him to do it, but he wouldn't.

> And he said unto his men, The LORD forbid
> that I should do this thing unto my master, the
> LORD's anointed, to stretch forth mine hand
> against him, seeing he is the anointed of the LORD.
> —1 Samuel 24:6

Saul was a worthless failure, but he was still the king and, in David's eyes, he was still God's anointed.

THE DANGER OF DIVISION

Later, when David ruled as king, another son of Belial tried to divide the kingdom.

> And there happened to be there a man of
> Belial, whose name was Sheba, the son of Bichri,
> a Benjamite: and he blew a trumpet, and said, We
> have no part in David, neither have we inheritance
> in the son of Jesse: every man to his tents, O Israel.
> So every man of Israel went up from after
> David, and followed Sheba the son of Bichri:
> but the men of Judah clave unto their king, from
> Jordan even to Jerusalem.
> —2 Samuel 20:1–2

Again, we see Belial at work through promoting a spirit of disrespect toward a man in legitimate authority.

I've never seen anyone get away with disrespecting or plotting against God's anointed. Three board members in Michigan tried to divide a church and turn the people against the young pastor. The young pastor was anointed of God. Every day, he prayed two hours for his church. People were being saved, lives were being changed, but the three board members didn't like him. They feared losing control of the church. They cast aspersions on his character and criticized his efforts. They constantly carped and criticized everything he did. One day they were flying their private airplane and it crashed. All three men were killed instantly.

Coincidence? Or had their behavior marked them for destruction?

*It's clear to me, when you are
seduced by Belial you become
marked for destruction.*

14

LADY FROM TULSA

In my mid-30s I experienced terrible pains in my chest. Once they persisted for eighteen months without relief. I would go home on Sunday nights feeling like I was dying. I remember telling my wife, "Good-bye. Tell the kids I love them." It felt like elephants were walking on my chest. I didn't ask anyone to pray for me, because I was trying to be the "man of faith." Nobody knew about this situation except Mary Jo and one nurse.

At that time, an evangelist named Lois lived in Tulsa, Oklahoma. I'd never heard of or met this woman, but God told her to pray for a pastor in Michigan who desperately needed help. She didn't know who or where this pastor was, but she got a flight into Grand Rapids, Michigan, and met with Jim Petersen, one of our missionaries. He didn't know I suffered with chest pain, but he called me anyway and asked if he could bring Lois over.

In 90 minutes, Lois was sitting in my office jibber jabbering about such weird things I thought she was crazy. She told us about a man whose voice box was removed due to cancer. She claimed she blew into his mouth and he regained his ability to speak. I tried to discern where she was coming from; I didn't get a bad feeling, but she seemed nutty.

Suddenly she jumped up, whirled my chair around, and threw her arms around me. I thought, "Now what! I'm sure glad Jim Petersen and Dave Snook, my associate pastor, are here. This woman is off her rocker." Lois had no earthly reason to know I was having chest pains, but she put her hand on my chest and prayed, "Father, in the Name of Jesus, I command healing to this heart and everything in it: the arteries, veins, valves, and muscle are now healed and made whole. Amen. There you go, honey, God sent me here for that." From that day to this, I have never felt another pain in my chest!

But she wasn't finished. She said to Dave Snook, "Honey, God wants to do something for you, too." She laid her hands on him and he fell to the floor, his conservative wing tips pointing straight up. He started shivering and crying, sweating and mumbling things we couldn't understand. Lois whispered to me that God was healing him of leukemia. I wondered if there was any way to prove it. Later, Dave did some family research and found that his grandpa and uncle both died of leukemia. It was quite possible that Dave had leukemia, even though it hadn't been diagnosed. In any case, he's alive and well today.

COURTROOM DRAMA

Later, we learned more about Lois. She attended a Catholic church, and when she accepted Jesus as her Savior and became filled with the Holy Spirit, she sparked revival in her congregation. One priest got saved and filled with the Holy Spirit, and he let Lois and her husband conduct weekday services. She held healing meetings at the Catholic Church.

A few people didn't like it, including a judge in the city. They plotted to get rid of Lois and her husband by sending a woman up for prayer who fell down and started screaming,

"My back! My back!" No X-ray or MRI showed any damage, but she sued Lois. The judge hearing the case, a member of the church, found Lois guilty and gave her a fine so large that she and her husband had to sell their house to pay it.

The day after the judge handed down his sentence, his son committed suicide. The following week, the judge went insane and was institutionalized.

It's clear to me, when you are seduced by Belial you become marked for destruction.

*We wrestle not against flesh and blood
but against spiritual powers
and principalities.*

15

DON'T MESS WITH GOD'S ANOINTED

David prayed against the sons of Belial.

> **O God, listen to my complaint. Protect my life from my enemies' threats.**
> **Hide me from the plots of this evil mob, from this gang of wrongdoers.**
> **They sharpen their tongues like swords and aim their bitter words like arrows.**
> **They shoot from ambush at the innocent, attacking suddenly and fearlessly.**
>
> —Psalm 64:1–4 (NLT)

Once, seven followers of Satan dressed in black robes came to our service to create problems, but they couldn't move their lips and sat spellbound. When I gave the altar call, six of them came forward and gave their lives to Jesus, and the very next week they were in the baptismal tank!

David's prayer continued:

> **They encourage each other to do evil and plan how to set their traps in secret. "Who will ever notice?" they ask.**
>
> —Psalm 64:5 (NLT)

It's funny how troublemakers think they won't get caught. I'm sure Judas Iscariot thought he wouldn't get caught—though he was always stirring up trouble behind the scenes. The prayer continues:

> As they plot their crimes, they say, "We have devised the perfect plan!" Yes, the human heart and mind are cunning.
>
> —Psalm 64:6 (NLT)

One of my associates was ministering to a demon-possessed transvestite and said, "You need the devil cast out of you." The demon spoke through the man and said, "What are you talking about? You have sins too." Sons and daughters of Belial try to focus attention on the sins of others to deflect attention from their own.

LAW OF THE BOOMERANG

I call this next line the law of the boomerang because while sinners shoot at you, God will suddenly shoot arrows at them, and they are the ones who get wounded.

> But God himself will shoot them with his arrows, suddenly striking them down.
>
> —Psalms 64:7 (NLT)

It's God who helps us resist Belial! We wrestle not against flesh and blood but against spiritual powers and principalities.

EVERY BATTLE

Right after the Jim Jones massacre in Jonestown, Guyana, in 1978, some members of Congress went on a witch hunt after legitimate television evangelists. They pulled Oral Roberts and Rex Humbard before a Senate committee. After the hearing, a government-appointed official said, "Humbard, I'm going to bring you and every other television evangelist down. I'm going to use every bit of influence I've got to put you out of business." Rex said, "You're forgetting one thing: God."

The next day that man went in for a simple dental treatment, and when they gave him a shot of Novocaine he dropped dead in the dental chair. The whole investigation was dropped.

My friend, Iver Frick, former superintendent of the Assemblies of God in Michigan, was driving through Nevada and went through a speed trap where they changed the limit from 60 to 50 after he went by. He went before the justice of the peace with his ticket and saw thousands of receipts from people who had to pay a fine from this speed trap. The greedy justice of the peace said, "That'll be one hundred dollars."

Brother Frick said, "I'm a man of God, pastor of a church, and I wouldn't lie to you. The speed sign said 60 not 50."

The justice of the peace laughed and said, "Prove it or go to jail."

Brother Frick paid the fine and said, "When I leave this place I'm going to call the governor."

The judge said, "Get out of here, preacher."

The next week, Brother Frick traveled back through the same town; he picked up a newspaper and saw the justice of the peace had been murdered. Was it a coincidence, or was that man marked for destruction for touching God's anointed?

As you will see, this trick of Belial is especially sinister when used against young people.

Jesus linked faith with authority. Kids who don't understand their parents' authority will be a problem in school, in church, and with the law."

16

FOR PARENTS

I love this little poem someone sent me. I've tried to discover who wrote it, but have not been able to find the author. My thanks to whoever wrote this clever poem.

My son came home from school one day,
with a smirk upon his face.
He decided he was smart enough
to put me in my place.

He said, "Guess what I learned in civics class
that's taught by Mr. Wright.
It's all about the laws today
and the children's bill of rights.

"It says I don't have to clean my room,
don't have to cut my hair.
No one can tell me what to think,
how to speak, or what to wear.

"I have freedom from religion,
and regardless of what you say,
I don't have to bow my head
and I sure don't have to pray.

"I can wear earrings if I want,
pierce my tongue and nose.
I can read and watch what I like
and be tattooed from head to toes.

"And if you ever spank me,
I'll charge you with a crime.
I'll back up all my charges
with the marks on my behind."

He said, "Don't you ever touch me,
this body's for my use,
not for your hugs and kisses,
that's just more child abuse.

"Don't preach about your morals,
like your momma did to you,
that's nothing but mind control
and it's illegal too.

"Mom, I have these children's rights
so you can't influence me,
or I'll call Children's Services,
better known as CSD."

Of course my natural instinct
was to toss him out the door,
but the chance to teach a lesson
made me think a little more.

I mulled it over carefully;
I couldn't let this go.
A little smile crept to my face;
he was messing with a pro.

Next day I took him shopping
at the local Goodwill store.
I told him, "Pick out all you want;
there are pants and shirts galore.

"I called and checked with CSD,
they said they didn't care
if I bought you K-Mart shoes
instead of Nike Air.

"And oh, I've cancelled that appointment
to take your driver's test.
The CSD is unconcerned,
so I'll decide what's best.

"No time to stop and eat,
or pick up stuff to munch.
And tomorrow you can start to learn
to make your own sack lunch.

"Just save that raging appetite
until dinner time,
we're having liver and onions;
it's a favorite dish of mine."

Then he asked, "Can we stop to rent a movie
I can watch on the VCR?"
"Sorry," I said, "I sold your TV
for new tires on my car.

"I also rented out your room;
you can take the couch instead.
CSD just requires that there's
a roof over your head.

"Your clothing won't be trendy now;
I'll choose the food we eat.
That allowance that you used to get
will buy me something neat.

"I'm selling off your Jet Ski,
dirt bike, and roller blades.
Check out the parent's bill of rights,
it's in effect today.

"Hey, hot shot, are you crying,
why are you on your knees?
Are you asking God to help?
Go call the CSD."

Parents, respecting authority starts at home! Your children can become mighty men and woman of God or they can become sons and daughters of Belial.

Jesus linked authority with true faith when the centurion said to Him:

> For I am a man under authority, having soldiers under me: and I say to this man, Go, and he goeth; and to another, Come, and he cometh; and to my servant, Do this, and he doeth it.
> When Jesus heard it, he marvelled, and said to them that followed, Verily I say unto you, I have not found so great faith, no, not in Israel.
> —Matthew 8:9–10

Jesus linked faith with authority. Kids who don't understand their parents' authority will be a problem in school, in church, and with the law. They will be more likely to end up in jail. Remember, the Fifth Commandment says to honor your father and mother that it may go well with you, and you will live a long time:

> Children, obey your parents in the Lord: for
> this is right.
>   Honour thy father and mother; which is the
> first commandment with promise;
>   That it may be well with thee, and thou mayest
> live long on the earth.
>
> —Ephesians 6:1–3

The Bible says in the last days many children won't respect their parents (2 Timothy 3:2), but that doesn't have to be true of you or your kids.

TWO DIFFERENT STORIES

I read a book entitled *Pursuing God's Best*, which tells the story of two girls at youth camp—Brenda and Stephanie. Both loved God, and both had problems with their imperfect parents. Brenda wouldn't accept her parents' authority. They were Christians, but they weren't perfect and she didn't like their rules, so she rejected their authority. She wasn't a bad girl, but she wanted to live her own way.

She met a guy named Jeff who wasn't saved. Perhaps she thought she'd lead him to the Lord, but she lost her virginity, started on drugs because she felt so guilty, and moved in with Jeff, who beat her severely. Her life went downhill fast, and it all began because she would not respect her parents' authority.

Stephanie's father wasn't saved. Stephanie wanted to go to an art college, but he thought that was silly and didn't want to pay her way. He would only pay if she agreed to go to a state college and study something "sensible." She felt crushed, but respected his will and prayed, "God, you know my desire is to study art, so help me to obey my father with a good attitude."

When it came time to send the money to the state college her dad called her downstairs. He had written out a check to the state college, but when he looked in her eyes something touched him. He ripped the check up and wrote out another to the art school instead.

Two different girls: one rebelled, one submitted. One got what she didn't want; the other girl's dream came true.

Parents: Teach your children to respect authority and you'll save them a lifetime of misery and failure. Only you have the power to do this in their early years. When they're older, it will be too late. Work hard to keep yourself and your children from susceptibility to Belial.

However, if you, or your family, should become ensnared, there is hope.

*You have the means—
and the authority—to
do extraordinary
things.*

17

BEATING BELIAL

We've seen how Belial works through false gods, sexual sin, and alcohol. We've seen how he is a source of confusion and disrespects authority.

Here's the good news. Jesus is greater than Belial or any other principality! Paul wrote:

> ...making mention of you in my prayers;
> That the God of our Lord Jesus Christ, the Father of glory, may give unto you the spirit of wisdom and revelation in the knowledge of him:
> The eyes of your understanding being enlightened; that ye may know what is the hope of his calling, and what the riches of the glory of his inheritance in the saints.
> And what is the exceeding greatness of his power to us-ward who believe, according to the working of his mighty power,
> Which he wrought in Christ, when he raised him from the dead, and set him at his own right hand in the heavenly places,
> Far above all principality, and power, and might, and dominion, and every name that is named, not only in this world, but also in that which is to come;
> And hath put all things under his feet, and gave him to be the head over all things to the church,

> **Which is his body, the fulness of him that**
> **filleth all in all.**
>
> —Ephesians 1:16b–23

We don't need to be dragged away and enticed. We don't need to be marked for destruction. Jesus said nothing shall by any means hurt us (Luke 10:19). In Isaiah 54:17 we're told that no weapon formed against us shall prosper—but only if we're walking with God in covenant.

The first and most important thing is to give your life to Jesus Christ, if you haven't already. After that you can torment the devil—just take this advice!

DON'T BE A PEW-WARMER

You must decide to be an extraordinary Christian. In Jesus' name, cast out devils and heal the sick, preach the Gospel, educate yourself, start a neighborhood Bible study— *do something.*

Children of Belial are passive. They want someone else to pray for them and fight their battles for them. Passivity is a form of defeat. The most battle-ready people are those already doing something for the Kingdom!

When Herod killed John the Baptist, Jesus felt sad but his response, even in that time of mourning, was to go to the next city and heal the sick (Matthew 14:14). Jesus was actively engaged in doing his Father's work!

Forget about being "too busy." You have the means— and the authority—to do extraordinary things. A young man named Larry was in a meeting when another man began shaking and crying. Larry discerned in the spirit that this man was bound, so Larry put his hand on his head and said, "In the Name of Jesus of Nazareth, be set free." That man fell over and said, "Thank you!" He had been bound by heroin, and God used the hands of an everyday Christian to free him.

> These miraculous signs will accompany those
> who believe: They will cast out demons in my
> name, and they will speak in new languages.
> —Mark 16:17 (NLT)

This verse applies to *every* believer, not just so-called "elite" believers.

THE LOYAL OPPOSITION

Do you want to torment the devil even more? Try this: Each time he tells you something, tell him the opposite. When he says, "You're worthless!" say, "I'm the apple of God's eye; I'm highly favored of the Lord." When he says, "You blew it!" say, "But if I confess my sins, God is faithful and just to forgive me and cleanse me from all unrighteousness."

Use the Word of God on Satan! When he says, "Be afraid because you are going to be destroyed!" say "Spirit of fear, God has not given you to me. You're trying to take away my sound mind. Be gone in the Name of Jesus!"

Then do yourself a favor and get into a prayer meeting. There is power in corporate prayer. Every believer should schedule both individual and corporate prayer times.

THE FIVE T'S

Years ago, an evangelist gave five "T's" for tormenting the devil and winning people to Christ.

The first "T" is tracts. The devil hates tracts. Millions of lives have been changed by little pamphlets about the Gospel. They use cute slogans or cartoons and may seem trivial, but they really work. Research shows for every tract you hand out, five people will read it and receive the Good News message.

The second "T" is tapes. Really, this "T" is now "CDs" since cassette tapes are obsolete. But the point is that some people don't like to read and prefer to receive information by hearing. So, giving someone a CD could be the best way to reach them. Many churches, including Mount Hope Church, have web sites where people can find sermons and other outreach messages that can be downloaded to MP3 players, or iPods. This is a great way to reach out to the lost.

The third "T" is talking to people. Get to know non-believers. Ask them what's going on in their lives. The Holy Spirit will give you words of knowledge and just the right words to touch their hearts.

The fourth "T" is testimony. Every born again person has a testimony. I decided whenever I go to a new church to speak, I give at least a three-minute testimony of how I met Jesus Christ. There is power in testifying to God's goodness. It seems to bind up devils and shut people's ears to anything but the Gospel. Your testimony can have the same effect, so tell it!

The fifth "T" is trumpeting. There comes a time when you need to trumpet, to boldly announce what God's Word says on the subject. For example, when the news headlines reflect what the Bible warned of: earthquakes, turmoil, increasing sinfulness, and perversion you can say, "Let me tell you what the Bible says about Belial and how he seduces people into sexual sin and perversion."

Trumpet the Word of God! Let Belial—and all of Satan's generals—hear the sound of their coming destruction. We're going to win this battle!

SECTION THREE

THE JEZEBEL SPIRIT

Christians get involved in witchcraft without even knowing it when they engage in sarcasm, ridicule, threats, and accusations.

18

THE SIN OF
WITCHCRAFT

Now let's look at the meaning of and spirit behind witchcraft. In some translations it means "sorcery." The sin of witchcraft springs from man's unregenerate nature—from flesh—not necessarily spirit. However, it quickly degenerates into demonic power if it is not checked.

The Bible says:

> **Now the works of the flesh are manifest, which are these; Adultery, fornication, uncleanness, lasciviousness,**
> **Idolatry, witchcraft....**
> **—Galatians 5:19–20a**

I used to teach that witchcraft was solely a work of the flesh because of this verse. But as I began to study God's Word, I found there are three levels of witchcraft and a powerful spirit promoting witchcraft among Christians. I don't think I would have believed it until I saw this principality at work.

Do I mean Christians are turning to sorcery, chanting curses, and making potions of bat's eyes and lizard tails? Not really, but we shouldn't be blind to the fact that real-life witches exist and continue to infiltrate churches.

A WITCH IN CHURCH

I was preaching in Portland, Michigan, a few years ago, and I strongly sensed in my spirit that Satan was at work in the service. It was like a big fan in the back of the auditorium kept blowing my words back at me. I felt I had to repeat them before anyone could hear what I was saying. A woman in the back of the auditorium sat with her head bowed. The Holy Spirit spoke to me and said, "She's the problem."

Afterwards, I pointed her out to the pastor and asked who she was, but he'd never seen her until that moment. I told him I believed she was a witch. When he approached her some time after that, he learned she was indeed a member of a coven of witches trying to disrupt church services in the Portland area. The good news is she ultimately gave her life to Jesus Christ!

The U.S. Armed Services estimates there are half a million people in the United States who practice Wicca, or witchcraft. This is not the peaceful, benign, pagan worshiping religion they want you to believe it is. Former witches have written books warning Christians about the diabolical plots they undertake to disrupt churches—charismatic churches in particular. Many practicing witches have infiltrated established churches and are controlling the pastor and congregation and causing great confusion.

One large church was destroyed after witches infiltrated it. The pastor yielded to a lustful, evil spirit. He committed adultery many times, and soon his wife became involved. Together, they introduced new doctrines to the congregation. They brought ballroom dancing into the sanctuary, and the pastor told the people to look into their partner's eyes until the Holy Spirit made a "connection."

Pastors, leaders, and deacons became involved as well, and they began swapping wives. Before long, divorce ran rampant.

Parishioners began having nervous breakdowns. The pastor's son committed suicide. His daughter divorced her husband and ran off with another man. One distraught young mother drowned her baby in the bathtub so the baby's soul would be "safe with Jesus," after her husband left her for another woman. Today that church is utterly destroyed because witchcraft slipped in.

MANIPULATION

In its first stage, witchcraft is more subtle and prevalent than neo-pagans in black robes brewing up potions and casting spells. Christians get involved in witchcraft without even knowing it when they engage in sarcasm, ridicule, threats, and accusations.

In the Hebrew, Greek, and Aramaic languages, a witch is a person who uses spoken words to harm or control others. At this level, witchcraft is simply manipulation. It is not about conjuring spirits or casting spells but it is about controlling people. Little phrases like, "If you really love me, you would do this," qualify as manipulation and witchcraft.

If you stick with this kind of witchcraft long enough it attracts a demon of witchcraft. Then you're no longer dealing with a work of the flesh but with a spiritual problem that is much harder to overcome.

The next level of witchcraft is actual sorcery and manipulates people through contact with the dark spiritual world. This is not as uncommon as you think. The 1-900-"psychic" numbers, tarot card readings, and horoscopes easily sucker people who crave spiritual power, even to the extent of trying to put curses on others.

I got an advertisement in the mail for a book called *Get Anyone to Do Anything: Never Feel Powerless Again*. This book promises to show you "secrets" of psychological manipulation that would make it possible for you to control and influence every situation and everyone around you. Each of us has a dark part down deep within us that wants to control other people and make them our puppets. But trying to overpower and control and manipulate others is the sin of witchcraft.

SHE-DEVIL

When I first entered the ministry, I never would have guessed that one of the devil's generals is assigned to lure Christians into witchcraft where they try to manipulate and control other Christians. But there is such a principality, and the Bible calls it Jezebel. Who is this principality?

I had always thought demons just hung around up in the rafters; I didn't realize they could attach themselves to people.

19

THE JEZEBEL SPIRIT

I mentioned a crisis I faced at the beginning of my pastoral ministry and how I learned about spiritual warfare. At that time I went toe-to-toe with the Jezebel spirit, though I only realized what actually happened years later.

I had rather naive notions before entering the ministry. I thought working among Christians would be the greatest experience because we would all be spiritual and we would all love God and we would all work together in harmony. However, after awhile I sensed something was wrong. Some people in our church worked not to promote God's plan but to frustrate it.

I was in the middle of a conflict with some church board members and some leadership over how to proceed with building our new worship center. God had spoken to me—and confirmed it in a number of other leaders—that we should not build until we had all the money in hand. Some didn't accept that word and were pressuring me to start building with the money we had. They wanted me to go to the bank and take out a mortgage. I found myself in a whirlwind of rumors, innuendo, false accusations, and slander—all because a certain group of so-called Christians (I called them the "Christian Mafia") thought they should control the church.

A man I once held in high regard came to my office to convince me to disobey God. "You're just the pastor; you look after spiritual matters. We control the business of the church," he said. "If you don't go along with us, I'm afraid that my family and I are going to have to withhold our tithe until you reconsider."

I didn't reconsider; I showed him the door! Then his son came to me in private and said, "My family has been in control for so long, and they feel like now they're losing that control. That's why they're acting the way they are." I told him I didn't want to be in control, that Jesus was the head of the church and the chairman of the board. Jesus had ruled on this matter. But the family was not swayed. A lust for power blinded them to the truth.

I started holding prayer meetings from 5:30 to 8:30 every morning, and my loyal staff of two joined me. We didn't know anything about the Jezebel spirit, but we started binding spirits of control. I had always thought demons just hung around up in the rafters; I didn't realize they could attach themselves to people. Soon, I received an avalanche of transfer requests from people wanting to move their membership to other churches. They didn't know that on some of those transfers I wrote notes to their next pastor about the trouble they'd caused.

YEARS LATER

Even then, I didn't fully recognize the spiritual power behind this rebellion. It was years later, when I felt something was blocking the church's progress, that I finally put a name to it. I gathered some of the key leaders in the church and told them I felt there was a spirit of competitiveness that was preventing us from reaching the heights God had for us. We prayed and repented, but there seemed to be something more—some "stopper" in the flow of God's blessings. I knew something bigger was hindering the vision, but it didn't have the identifying traits of Leviathan, Mammon, or Belial.

Then a trusted friend gave me a video concerning a particular spirit on the loose against the church, particularly in America. After that, I saw a CBN television special concerning this same spirit. Finally, I read *The Jezebel Spirit* by Francis Frangipane. At last I realized the spirit that had infiltrated our church all those years ago, and that was currently frustrating the flow of blessings in our church had a name: Jezebel.

BIBLE BASIS

Jezebel first appears in 1 Kings, and then again in the book of Revelation. Jesus mentioned her by name when he spoke to the church in Thyatira:

> …These things saith the Son of God, who hath his eyes like unto a flame of fire, and his feet are like fine brass; [Note: "eyes" is a symbol of discernment; "brass" is a symbol of judgment].
>
> I know thy works, and charity, and service, and faith, and thy patience, and thy works; and the last to be more than the first.
>
> Notwithstanding I have a few things against thee, because thou sufferest that woman Jezebel, which calleth herself a prophetess, to teach and to seduce my servants to commit fornication, and to eat things sacrificed unto idols.
> —Revelation 2:18b–20

Was Jesus referring to an actual woman in the church named Jezebel? I think that's very unlikely. Rather, he was identifying the spirit behind that individual, "which calleth herself a prophetess."

She wasn't a prophetess, but she called herself one. She donned the robes of authority but did not have true authority—which only comes from God.

I believe Jesus was speaking about "spiritual" fornication because in Psalms God likens idolatry to whoring.

**Thus were they defiled with their own works,
and went a whoring with their own inventions.**
—Psalm 106:39

Let's stop here and ask, what did Jesus mean by referring to her as Jezebel? Why would He bring up the wife of an Old Testament king? It's to give us a clue into the nature of the Jezebel spirit, which so clearly appears in the life of the original Jezebel—the wife of Ahab, scourge of Israel.

Each of us, under certain circumstances, at one time or another, is capable of manipulative and controlling behavior.

20

THE BAD NEWS QUEEN

Every person and story in the Old Testament was given to teach a spiritual truth. The men and women actually lived, but their actions and stories direct us how to live—or how not to live

Look at the real person Jezebel in the Bible, and you'll find the characteristics of the spirit of Jezebel that Satan still uses as a weapon against God's people today.

The historical Jezebel was married to Ahab, a whiny, spineless king who did more evil in the sight of God than any other king before him. As bad as Ahab was, he was nothing compared to his wife who didn't care who was king—she was determined to be in control. Remember this: the spirit of Jezebel is a spirit of domination and control.

Everything about the Jezebel spirit goes back to that root. She doesn't care who is the rightful king, president, pastor, leader, or anointed individual. She lusts after power and is wickedly clever in getting it. We're told:

> **But there was none like unto Ahab, which did sell himself to work wickedness in the sight of the LORD, whom Jezebel his wife stirred up.**
> **—1 Kings 21:25**

Jezebel systematically killed God's true prophets because their legitimate authority was a threat to her illegitimate authority.

> **For it was so, when Jezebel cut off the prophets of the LORD, that Obadiah took an hundred prophets, and hid them by fifty in a cave....**
> **—1 Kings 18:4a**

The very first time Jezebel is mentioned in Scripture, she established the worship of false gods in Israel. She introduced Baal and his consort Ashtoreth—the male and female fertility "gods" of the Canaanites and Syrians. She brought in 450 prophets of Baal, and 400 prophets of Ashtoreth. In reality, they were just puppets to do her bidding. Elijah and his followers eventually slaughtered these prophets on Mount Carmel when God sent fire from Heaven.

Throughout her life Jezebel showed a total disregard for anyone who stood in her way. When Elijah killed her prophets, she sent a message to him that she wouldn't rest until he was dead. In her words:

> **...So let the gods do to me, and more also, if I make not thy life as the life of one of them by to morrow about this time.**
> **—1 Kings 19:2b**

Later, she callously killed a man on a whim. Naboth had a vineyard close to Ahab's palace that Ahab wanted to buy. But Naboth had plans for the property and wouldn't sell it. Ahab did a very kingly thing: he pouted.

> **And Ahab came into his house heavy and displeased because of the word which Naboth the Jezreelite had spoken to him: for he had said, I will not give thee the inheritance of my fathers. And he**

laid him down upon his bed, and turned away his
face, and would eat no bread.
But Jezebel his wife came to him, and said
unto him, Why is thy spirit so sad, that thou
eatest no bread?

—1 Kings 21:4–5

When Ahab told her of Naboth's refusal to sell his land
she responded:

…Dost thou now govern the kingdom of Israel?
arise, and eat bread, and let thine heart be merry: I
will give thee the vineyard of Naboth the Jezreelite.

—1 Kings 21:7b

She wrote a letter in Ahab's name and sealed it with his
seal, ordering Naboth's death. In it she wrote detailed instructions about how to carry out the "hit" on Naboth:

And she wrote in the letters, saying, Proclaim a
fast, and set Naboth on high among the people:
And set two men, sons of Belial, before him,
to bear witness against him, saying, Thou didst
blaspheme God and the king. And then carry him
out, and stone him, that he may die.

—1 Kings 21:9b–10

That's exactly what happened. Then, in an almost casual
tone, she told Ahab.

And it came to pass, when Jezebel heard that
Naboth was stoned, and was dead, that Jezebel said
to Ahab, Arise, take possession of the vineyard of
Naboth the Jezreelite, which he refused to give thee
for money: for Naboth is not alive, but dead.

—1 Kings 21:15

The Jezebel spirit sees people as pawns, not living human beings who have feelings and dreams and goals. If she can use them, and then cast them aside, she'll do it. She thinks nothing of exceeding her authority for self-serving reasons, or taking things that do not belong to her, like Naboth's vineyard.

END GAME

Jezebel's ultimate goal is to kill God's true work, wherever it springs up. She comes against people in legitimate spiritual authority. In fact, almost every time a man of true spiritual authority was raised up in the Bible, a Jezebel was right there to oppose him. In First Kings, Jezebel did her best to try to kill Elijah.

Centuries later, John the Baptist came in the spirit and power of Elijah and was opposed by Herodias, wife of Herod, acting under the guidance of the Jezebel spirit. John the Baptist called people to repent just as Elijah had, and this upset Herodias who manipulated her husband into making a foolish agreement that got John beheaded (Matthew 14).

Judas Iscariot, perhaps under the influence of the Jezebel spirit, craved control and wanted to set the course for Jesus' ministry. He couldn't wait and let God do things according to plan, so he tried to manipulate the situation to his own advantage. He wanted to get Jesus to lead a revolt against Rome and set up a kingdom in which Judas would help rule. The very thing he wanted—power—he lost. But the disciples who stayed with Jesus were given supernatural power over demon spirits, sickness, and all the powers of darkness!

Even today, the Jezebel spirit comes against God's legitimate authority wherever it is found. This includes not just pastors but anyone following the call of God—even you.

CONTROL!

Jezebel is hell-bent on controlling other people. When a wife wants to control her husband—that's Jezebel. When a husband demands submission from his wife—that's Jezebel. It doesn't matter what tools they use—intimidation, fear, manipulation, threats, bribery—the bottom line is control.

Jezebel doesn't have a gender, even though it's convenient to refer to it as a "she." It strikes both women and men, and it brings such a deep darkness and deception that before you realize it you are ensnared. Other people can see it in you, but you can't. Others perceive you're manipulative, controlling, hard to be around, but you make excuses and find ways to cast the blame away from you.

Some people reading this book—perhaps you—have felt so controlled or manipulated by others that you hardly trust anyone. The spirit of Jezebel working through other people—even Christians and church leaders—has bullied you. Perhaps you have made a practice of manipulating others, either through intimidation, fear, or sweet talk. You may think it's "cute" or beneficial, but any kind of spiritual or emotional manipulation is wrong.

Some wives want so badly to see their husbands saved that they actually try to manipulate them and unwittingly come into partnership with the spirit of Jezebel. This spirit actually keeps their husbands away from God. There are husbands who use intimidation to make their wives submit. Rather than motivating by love, they try to motivate by coercion.

WHO'S SUSCEPTIBLE

Who's prone to practice witchcraft and come under the sway of a Jezebel spirit? Each of us, under certain circumstances, at one time or another, is capable of manipulative

145

and controlling behavior. We all err and try to bend people for our own selfish purpose. Here are five things that may lead people to become susceptible to the Jezebel spirit.

1. People with major insecurities.

Any person, Christian or otherwise, who has not found his or her true value in Christ has an endless need for approval. This often drives him or her to control other people to attain at least the feeling of being in control.

2. People obsessed with controlling others.

Some people are on a huge power trip. They are fascinated by the idea of "playing god" and enjoy the feeling of making someone else do their will. They will even try psychic or supernatural powers to play their game, which amuses them and makes them feel powerful.

3. People who lack courage to be straightforward.

It's difficult to be sincere and honest at all times because sometimes honesty offends people, and then they don't like you. Some can't handle this, so they resort to manipulation in order to gain favor and friends.

4. People trying to maintain a position of illegitimate authority.

Some people have gained positions of authority by fleshly means, and they live in fear of true spiritual authority. They're afraid they will be found out and stripped of power, so they launch pre-emptive strikes against anyone who smells like a threat.

This was the case of Diotrephes (3 John 1:9) who loved a position of preeminence in the church. If he couldn't sit up front and get the glory he wasn't happy. When John pointed out his sin, Diotrephes responded with stiff-necked pride. He became a prater whose foolishly babbling words poisoned the church—a witch. He began to deal in witchcraft when his seat of power was threatened.

5. People who are dissatisfied and ungrateful. A wife who fantasizes about having a more spiritual husband is susceptible to the Jezebel spirit. She may trick him into attending prayer meetings or pout about his lack of spiritual understanding. A man who can't govern his own household is susceptible and may try to gain power through manipulation rather than true spiritual authority, which comes from obeying God and being humble.

What are the Jezebel spirit's tactics? What are the weapons it uses against us? How do you know if this particular spirit is coming against your life? Let's find out.

The shield of faith will quench Jezebel's arrows before they sting you!

21

DISCOURAGEMENT

For almost four years, I was tormented by a man who showed up in my office every Monday morning to let me know everything I did wrong in service the day before. I dreaded seeing him because he was such a critic. Sometimes after he left I felt so discouraged that I wondered if I was helping or harming the church.

I now know discouragement is a tactic of the Jezebel spirit. She used it on Elijah when he had a great miracle from God and slew eight hundred and fifty false prophets. In his moment of triumph, she leveled an attack and said she'd have him killed within twenty-four hours. Elijah ran for his life from this demon-possessed woman (1 Kings 19).

It doesn't make sense, does it? This great prophet of God hiding under a juniper tree, telling himself how worthless he was. And yet anyone who's ever preached or taught knows how vulnerable you feel after bringing the Word to people. The devil climbs all over you, telling you how badly you did. If ten people were saved, you think it should have been twenty. You remember the lady who wasn't paying attention or the man in the back reading a book, and not the hundreds who joined in whole-hearted worship. It's terribly easy to discourage a preacher right after a service.

In prison, John the Baptist got so discouraged he sent two of his men to ask Jesus if He really was the Messiah. The

Jezebel spirit had him so down that he doubted Jesus! See Matthew 11:2–3.

STINGERS

You don't have to be a preacher to come under this kind of attack. Jezebel comes against every believer. Often the discouragement comes packaged as a sly comment that includes a stinger designed to get your mind off God and on to a problem that you shouldn't be worrying about. Let me give an example.

Once I was on vacation with my family at a little cabin up north on a lake. There was no telephone and no running water. It was a wonderful place to relax, and I fished the days away.

When I returned home I learned a man in our church had died. He came occasionally and didn't seem rooted, but his wife was very active in ministry and seemed to be a mature Christian. She held a position as a volunteer phone operator. As soon as I got home, I called her to give my condolences and she said, "We needed you, and you weren't here."

That may not sound like much, but the comment had a little stinger in it. I started feeling guilty for something I shouldn't have felt guilty about. That simple statement discouraged me—it was really a Jezebel attack.

Then I discovered this woman was using her volunteer phone operator sessions to spread rumors and lies about me. I called her into my office and told her I knew she was spreading gossip, and she said, "People just tell me things. I don't know why they feel comfortable telling me things."

I snapped back, "Birds of a feather flock together." I removed her from her phone ministry, and she left the church in a huff. She was dealing in witchcraft.

Do You Laugh Or Cry?

Stingers can come from anywhere, and their effect can last a long time. Maybe somebody said something to you in high school that still haunts you. Maybe a parent said something when you were a child, and the stinger went deep and still is a source of discouragement for you.

I heard a story about a man and his wife who walked into a pet store. The parrot at the door said, "Hey buddy, your wife sure is ugly and she smells bad too. She doesn't even know how to dress!" The wife started to cry and the husband told the store manager that the parrot had offended them. The store manager went over and smacked the parrot and said, "Don't tell the truth like that to the customers!"

It's easy to laugh off some negative comments. My wife Mary Jo can tell me my socks look goofy, but that doesn't wound my spirit, I know she's teasing in fun. However, other stingers are mean-spirited witchcraft; their points drive deep into the soul where they continue to release their poison.

I used to get unsigned notes that contained stingers. They might take Scripture out of context and use it to criticize something I said or did. I wanted to respond, but I didn't know who to respond to. Sometimes when I prayed, my mind returned to these hurtful comments. Finally, God told me not to read any unsigned letters because they are from the devil, designed to harm, control, or manipulate. When I quit reading them, I became much more focused and didn't have to deal with as many of Jezebel's darts.

Use The Shield!

Many years ago, I found out a group from our church was holding prayer meetings to ask God to remove me from the pastorate—or kill me! That was a pretty discouraging bit of news, but it didn't hurt too badly because I knew they were essentially dabbling in witchcraft, and their desires would come to nothing. Once, God spoke to false prophets and said:

> Because with lies ye have made the heart of the righteous sad, whom I have not made sad; and strengthened the hands of the wicked, that he should not return from his wicked way, by promising him life:
> Therefore ye shall see no more vanity, nor divine divinations: for I will deliver my people out of your hand: and ye shall know that I am the LORD.
> —Ezekiel 13:22–23a

Needless to say, God protected me!

Have you ever been "stung?" Has someone ruined your day with a comment that contained a stinger? Has someone tried to make you feel guilty in order to control you? Has someone ever said something that bothered you and you didn't know why? That's when you know the spirit of Jezebel is at work, sowing discouragement and trying to manipulate and control.

We can't control what other people say to us, but we can control our response to it. Paul wrote about the shield of faith:

> Above all, taking the shield of faith, wherewith ye shall be able to quench all the fiery darts of the wicked.
> And take the helmet of salvation, and the sword of the Spirit, which is the word of God...
>
> —Ephesians 6:16–17

The shield of faith will quench Jezebel's arrows before they sting you! If a stinger pierces you and pumps its poison into your spirit, it could grow into a root of bitterness. Then you would pick up the spirit of witchcraft and try to control the person who made you feel bad in the first place! It's best to hold up the shield of faith, stick to what you believe, and let those arrows fall to the ground.

How should we deal with Jezebel's stingers? With faith! When someone says, "You're a loser!" You respond, "No, I'm not. I'm more than a conqueror through Jesus who loves me!" (Romans 8:37). When Jezebel tries to control you with lies and manipulation, you defend yourself with your faith in God's promises and the spoken word of the Scriptures.

There are other techniques of manipulation the Jezebel spirit uses to accomplish the goal of controlling you.

People dealing in witchcraft are often attracted to two kinds of ministry: intercession and prophecy.

22

COUNTERFEIT REVELATION

At the end of service one Sunday, I was walking out the foyer door when a woman approached me. She was dressed nicely and appeared normal.

"Hello," she said. "My name is Leann (not her real name), and I'm a prophet."

"You are?" I responded.

"Yes. I heard you announce that members of your church are going on a mission's trip to Venezuela. You have to stop that trip because ten of the people will be killed—assassinated by terrorists."

"Oh?" I replied.

"Yes," she said, "and you'll know that I'm a true prophet because an earthquake is coming to Michigan before December 13."

I thanked her and walked away. Then I wrote down everything she said and prayed about the trip to Venezuela. God assured me it would be a great trip. Indeed, everyone went and came home safely. December 13 came and went and there was no earthquake. Then I got a letter from Leann that read, "Thus saith the Lord. My son, I am now going to bring you home before your time because you refuse to accept my servant as a true prophet."

I wrote back and said, "I do believe you are a prophet—a false prophet. Sincerely, Pastor Williams."

TWO ATTRACTIVE MINISTRIES

People dealing in witchcraft are often attracted to two kinds of ministry: intercession and prophecy. In both you have occasion to speak on God's behalf, and both can become power bases for people with the Jezebel spirit to try and control a church. Both of these ministries are vital to church life, but both are open to the abuse of witchcraft. Remember Jesus said of "Jezebel:"

> Notwithstanding I have a few things against thee, because thou sufferest that woman Jezebel, which calleth herself a prophetess, to teach and to seduce my servants to commit fornication, and to eat things sacrificed unto idols.
> —Revelation 2:20

I'm wary of anyone who calls himself or herself a prophet. It may be true, but one of the proofs comes from discerning the spirit at work through their ministry.

There's a man who calls me every once in awhile with a prophetic message, and he's always accurate. There's nothing I like more than a genuine word from the Lord given by somebody who loves me and wants to share God's mind on a matter. But there's nothing more bitter than a so-called word that comes from the spirit of witchcraft.

In some of the meetings at our church, we used to have microphones on the floor. If a person had a prophetic word they could come forward and share it with everyone. However, I found the true prophets were too humble to get up and talk; the false ones, though, were never afraid to speak.

Once, a woman prophesied and something didn't feel right about it. I tracked her down and found out she was single, pregnant, and claiming it was an immaculate conception. I banned her from prophesying.

Another woman would storm up to the microphone and say things like, "My people, I love you with an everlasting love, but you only think your names are in the Book of Life. If you don't work for me, your name will not be there!" People would clap and receive it, but to me it felt vindictive. So I called her in to the office and found she was bitter from past hurts and was prophesying out of her own anger. I told her not to prophesy any more, and she started a mini-revolt against me.

People said I was anti-Pentecostal and wanted to turn our church into a Catholic church. One man got up and prophesied, "Thus saith the Lord, I say unto thee thou art making policies against my Spirit and I am not pleased. Make thee no policy against my Spirit; give my Spirit free reign, saith God. For thou art quenching the Spirit." It was a deliberate false prophecy with the goal to force me to allow these Jezebels to spew their lies and manipulations.

The Jezebel spirit always seems to maneuver into leadership positions or a trusted place in the intercessory prayer ministry. A pastor at one of our daughter churches went through a Jezebel situation when an intercessor began claiming that the attack on the World Trade Center was the judgment of God on America. The pastor demurred and said it had all the fingerprints of the devil; God wasn't mad at America. The pastor pointed out we still have the largest number of ministries and prayer networks the world has ever seen, and God wants us to succeed in our mission.

This intercessor rebelled and passed out photocopied prophecies to other people, end-running the pastor's authority. She thought she'd heard from God, but her actions reflected a Jezebel spirit and didn't do anyone any good.

Some counterfeit intercessors or prophets say they've heard from God about somebody else. They try to tell you what God supposedly said about this person. Anytime that happens, you know you've run into the Jezebel spirit. God deals with individuals directly. He does not gossip! When Nathan the prophet got a word from God about David's sin, he went directly to David and said, "You are the man" (see 2 Samuel 12: 1–7).

Anybody who says, "I was praying and I got a word about Frank, but don't tell Frank," is influenced by a Jezebel spirit. All you have to do is say, "No, you miserable Jezebel. I mark you. You are not an intercessor or a prophet."

Even as a pastor I don't want to hear rumors or so-called "words" about other people. I've got a rule that if you know something, and you haven't been to the person involved, don't even think about coming to me. If you think you've got an accusation against an elder or a pastor, you'd better make sure there are at least two or three witnesses because I don't want to hear your dream, your revelation, or your false prophecy. I've no respect for those who flow in the Jezebel spirit.

Watch out for counterfeiters who claim to speak for God. Hold true prophets and intercessors in the high esteem they deserve, but push away any Jezebel-inspired "words" from God.

There are still other ways the Jezebel spirit works.

When the witchcraft-loving, God-hating, ugly, manipulating, controlling, evil spirit of Jezebel is around, nobody has peace.

23

MORE OF JEZEBEL'S WEAPONS

Another sign of the Jezebel spirit at work is lack of peace. The Bible says:

> And it came to pass, when Joram saw Jehu, that he said, Is it peace, Jehu? And he answered, What peace, so long as the whoredoms of thy mother Jezebel and her witchcrafts are so many?
>
> —2 Kings 9:22

When the witchcraft-loving, God-hating, ugly, manipulating, controlling, evil spirit of Jezebel is around, nobody has peace. There's a continual condition of strife. She thrives in a chaotic, topsy-turvy environment.

FLATTERY

Flattery is Jezebel's powerfully seductive weapon.

A man caught me after service one day and said, "The anointing was all over you today. As I looked into the spirit world, I saw rain coming down out of Heaven all over you as you preached."

As he said it, something inside me felt sick. Flattery is the anti-Christ's method, we're told in Daniel. He comes flattering everyone. It turns out the man wanted to worm his way into the church to control us. I'm thankful we were able to discern his intentions and resist them.

Who can resist a kind word? Even an enemy can make himself attractive by saying all the right things. When the prophet Jehu paid Jezebel a visit she dolled herself up and batted her eyes, trying to flatter and seduce him even though he came to prophesy her doom.

> **And when Jehu was come to Jezreel, Jezebel heard of it; and she painted her face, and tired her head, and looked out at a window.**
> —2 Kings 9:30

If Jezebel can't seduce you with her looks, she'll try to win your confidence. The Jezebel spirit says things like, "You're the only one I can talk to about this. I'm only telling you this because I can trust you."

We had a Jezebel spirit develop over time in a man on our board. He said the most hateful things about everyone in authority, from the president of the United States on down. Then he started railing against television preachers. That year I took a three-month sabbatical, and he told a number of people I had stolen ten thousand dollars from the church! Our elder called him in, along with all the people he had talked to, sat them around the table in the boardroom and said, "I suspect that this man has come to each of you telling you that you're the only one that he can trust." Their eyes went wide, and they realized they'd been duped—flattered by the spirit of Jezebel. Some ended up leaving the church, but most stayed.

When someone comes to you claiming they are confiding in you alone, you'd better believe there are a dozen more people they've said that to. Jezebel thrives on building pride in people because then they are easily seduced.

FALSE TEARS

People with the Jezebel spirit know how to turn on the tears. They pretend to be hurt and are easily offended, but it's a trap! Their tears are meant to manipulate you, just like children who cry when they don't get their way—and as soon as you give in, the tears instantly shut off.

BACK-AND-FORTH EMOTIONAL OUTBURSTS

The Jezebel spirit causes unpredictable emotional outbursts—one minute mean and the next nice. This is exactly the brainwashing technique the North Koreans used during the Korean War. One day they were extremely cruel to the prisoners, and the next they were extremely nice—back and forth. This technique so confused the prisoners they became docile and incapable of independent thought.

The point is Jezebel keeps you off balance and wins the battle for control.

GUILT TRIPS

You've heard people say, "You owe me." The Jezebel spirit keeps track of favors so she can use them in the future. This is what Absalom did when he betrayed his father David. He sat at the city gate giving favors to people, acting sorry for them and patting them on the back. When he wanted their support to overthrow David, he called in his favors (2 Samuel 15).

Once, our church had to remove the pastor of a daughter church who was flowing in false doctrine. He said, "After sixteen years of love and service, this is how I'm repaid?" He wanted to "guilt" us into letting him keep control.

PULLING THE PURSE STRINGS

Jezebel tries to control through money. Often people with the Jezebel spirit will give lots of money to a church, not to bless but to control. I know of a church where a man with a Jezebel spirit sat on the board and had driven off every pastor. He was arrogant and bought cars for the presbyter's son to curry favor. Finally, the church rose up against him and he said, "Fine. I'll take my money and go!" So instead of getting rid of him they decided to get rid of the latest pastor.

SYMPATHY

Jezebel plays on your sympathy saying, "Poor old me. I got a raw deal." People using this tactic are usually very general in their complaints. They can't tell you anything specific that was done to them, and they can't tell you specific names of people—but still they want your sympathy.

The Jezebel spirit is fiercely independent and viciously fights for preeminence. The only time she will appear submissive or servant-like is for the sake of gaining some strategic advantage. Watch out for pity parties.

SELECTIVE INFORMATION

Jezebel spirits tell you only a small part of the matter to manipulate you. A man used to tell me, "A lot of people are upset about what you did." This intimidated me for a while, but then I learned to say, "Give me the names of those people." He'd say, "I wouldn't feel comfortable giving you names." Finally he stopped saying it altogether because he didn't really have any names—except for maybe his own! He was giving selective information to try and control me.

John said to test the spirits to see if they're of God.

> Beloved, believe not every spirit, but try the spirits whether they are of God: because many false prophets are gone out into the world.
> —1 John 4:1

When we were refinancing one of our daughter churches, they asked us to co-sign on their mortgage. I already had discerned some troublesome things about this church's pastor, and I was leery about this situation. I went to the closing at the bank and read over the paperwork. I noticed it said this pastor would hold the deed to the property, but my church would be responsible for the note to pay it off. I turned to the bank vice president and asked,

"If we're putting a hundred thousand dollars on the line, why aren't we on the deed? We've always been on the deeds of our other daughter church properties."

The vice president said, "That's what the pastor told me to do."

I refused to sign, and later we found out this pastor had been planning for months to defect and would have taken the church property with him and left us holding the bill. He had a Jezebel spirit, a spirit of control, which led him to give us selective information to try and hide his real intentions.

THREATS

Jezebel's last resort is to threaten. She threatened Elijah, John the Baptist, and every other great man or woman of God. She will threaten you, but you can stand up to her and say, "No! I don't believe you for one minute." Don't be like Elijah who took her threat seriously and ran into the desert to hide under a bush. Remember her threats are empty. She doesn't have the power to enforce them. The only power she has is to trick you and lie to you and get you to believe her manipulations. Don't let her succeed. Stand strong in faith and God's promises.

*It's hard to break loose of a Jezebel spirit.
But there comes a point when
every one of us must
stand up to her....*

24

JEZEBEL'S GRISLY FATE

What happened to the real Jezebel? What will happen to people with the Jezebel spirit? Read on but be warned, the answer is not pretty.

You remember Jezebel tried to seduce and flatter Jehu the prophet by putting on makeup, doing her hair, and perching in a window to wait for him. Here's how she met her end.

> And as Jehu entered in at the gate, she said,
> Had Zimri peace, who slew his master?
> And he lifted up his face to the window, and said, Who is on my side? who? And there looked out to him two or three eunuchs.
> —2 Kings 9:31–32

These eunuchs were pip-squeaks Jezebel thought she had under her control, but they betrayed her.

> And he said, Throw her down. So they threw her down: and some of her blood was sprinkled on the wall, and on the horses: and he trode her under foot.
> And when he was come in, he did eat and drink, and said, Go, see now this cursed woman, and bury her: for she is a king's daughter.
> And they went to bury her: but they found no more of her than the skull, and the feet, and the palms of her hands.

> Wherefore they came again, and told him. And
> he said, This is the word of the LORD, which he
> spake by his servant Elijah the Tishbite, saying,
> In the portion of Jezreel shall dogs eat the flesh of
> Jezebel:
> And the carcase of Jezebel shall be as dung upon
> the face of the field in the portion of Jezreel; so
> that they shall not say, This is Jezebel.
> —2 Kings 9:33–37

She became like dung in a field. What a fitting end for a disgusting woman. Unfortunately, the spirit that motivated her is alive and at work in the world today.

THE END OF THE ROAD

People who harbor a Jezebel spirit will have a terrible ending. Jesus said:

> And I gave her space to repent of her fornica-
> tion; and she repented not.
> Behold, I will cast her into a bed, and them that
> commit adultery with her into great tribulation,
> except they repent of their deeds.
> And I will kill her children with death; and
> all the churches shall know that I am he which
> searcheth the reins and hearts: and I will give unto
> every one of you according to your works.
> —Revelation 2:21–23

Isn't that an awful thought? God will cut off the lineage of people who cooperate with Jezebel. But to those who resist, Jesus promises:

> And he that overcometh, and keepeth my
> works unto the end, to him will I give power
> over the nations:
> —Revelation 2:26

To those who don't fall prey to Jezebel, God will give true spiritual authority.

> **And he shall rule them with a rod of iron; as the vessels of a potter shall they be broken to shivers: even as I received of my Father.**
> **And I will give him the morning star.**
> —Revelation 2:27–28

This means when Satan sets up his strongholds, you're going to shatter them to bits with true spiritual authority that comes from being under the Father's authority.

It's hard to break loose of a Jezebel spirit. But there comes a point when every one of us must stand up to her—whether it's a spirit stuck on us or a spirit operating against us through another person. But how do we do it?

BASIC BATTLE PLAN

Here's the plan for defeating Jezebel. These are weapons she can't withstand.

1. Repentance and Humility

One of my frequent prayers is, "God, without you I can do nothing. Unless you build the house, I labor in vain." That is the cornerstone for everything I do.

You never see humility in someone controlled by the Jezebel spirit, unless it's false humility designed to manipulate. You won't see Jezebel on her knees at the altar because Jezebel doesn't believe in repentance. You won't hear her say, "I was wrong, and I'm sorry."

I used to have a hot temper. One time I was upset with one of the church's employees, and I exploded. I threw a pen, yelled and screamed, pushed him, and stormed into his office and accidentally knocked a hole in the wall. I realized how foolishly I was behaving, and within ten minutes I was begging his forgiveness.

Another time, I got really frustrated and angry at my accountant. I kicked a wastebasket, yelled at her, and fired her! Ten minutes later I hired her back and asked her forgiveness. These days I don't blow up like that, but I'm imperfect in other ways. Everyone is. God does not expect you to be perfect, but he does expect you to repent quickly when you've done the wrong thing.

Repentance and humility will drive the spirit of Jezebel out of your life.

2. Submit To God's Spiritual Authority

In 1 Samuel 15:23, the Bible says rebellion is as the sin of witchcraft. When we rebel against God's delegated authority we are rebelling against God. That's why God said to Samuel not to take criticism personally because they were speaking against God, not Samuel. Jesus said in John 15 that if the world hated him it would also hate us. When Paul persecuted the Church, Jesus confronted him and said:

> ...Saul, Saul, why persecutest thou me?
> —Acts 9:4b

When somebody comes against you it's because they hate Jesus, but there's no better place to be than under his legitimate authority. James 4 tells us to submit ourselves to God. It's the only way to be completely free of counterfeit authority.

A submitted heart means trusting God for daily things. One time I was charged for flood insurance by a bank that held my mortgage. But I already had flood insurance, so I sent them proof. I got a letter back saying they had charged my credit card for flood insurance—and this was their own credit card that I'd never activated! I wrote a letter threatening to take them to small claims court and make their lives miserable, and I felt so justified!

At the same time, I was waiting for my tax refund. Even though my kids and I filed our tax returns on the same day, they got their refunds and I didn't.

I realized that I was feeling out of control and was in danger of giving in to a spirit of control. So I laid it out before the Lord and said, "I don't want to have anything to do with the Jezebel spirit. I don't want to feel like I've got to control, manipulate, or make those people do what's right in my own strength. I'm going to send them a nice letter asking if they want to charge me for flood insurance or have me as a customer for life."

It was so liberating to trust God. That week I got my tax refund check and a letter from the bank saying they'd removed the charge for flood insurance from my credit card. Hallelujah! I couldn't have done it better myself.

3. Plead the Blood of Jesus

This may sound strange, but one of the most powerful practices in my life is, when I first get up in the morning, the first thing I do is pray, "Father, I plead the blood of Jesus over my life, spirit, mind, and body; over Mary Jo's life, spirit, mind, and body; over Trina's life, spirit, mind, and body; over David's life, spirit, mind, and body; over my family, Mary Jo's family, over our membership, our leaders, prayer partners, students...." I go right down the list which takes me less than a minute. The Bible says in Revelation 12:11 they overcame by the blood of the Lamb and the word of their testimony. The blood of Jesus is powerful enough to protect me from the spirit of witchcraft!

If it sounds like an old, stodgy, Pentecostal practice, I don't care. It works.

4. Use the Testimony of God's Word

The second part of Revelation 12:11 says that they over-came by the word of their testimony, which is the spoken Word of God. When Jesus fought off the devil, he used the Word of God (Matthew 4). No matter what form the devil comes to you in—the Jezebel spirit, Belial, Leviathan, Mammon, or anything else—you must speak only God's Word. Don't rely on what you think or a rumor you heard. Use the testimony of God's Word! It'll slice and dice the Jezebel spirit and send her fleeing.

5. Strongly Resist

First Peter 5:8 says:

> **Be sober, be vigilant; because your adversary
> the devil, as a roaring lion, walketh about, seeking
> whom he may devour:**

To strongly resist means don't put up with even a tiny bit of Jezebel's work. Come right out and boldly oppose it whenever it pops up.

A strong woman of faith was approached by someone who said, "Let me tell you what's wrong with this church." She responded, "Do my ears look like garbage cans to you? This church saved my life. I met Jesus and was filled with the Holy Spirit here. Don't even try to tell me anything bad about my church."

I love that. She didn't give the devil an inch, and that's my final advice to you on this topic: Do not tolerate Jezebel, even for one minute. She cannot be negotiated with, pleased, or appeased. Yes, we all get in the flesh every once in a while and try to control somebody. That doesn't mean the Jezebel spirit possesses us, but if it becomes a way of life you'd better believe there's a spirit involved. True authority liberates, not dominates; it motivates by love, not fear.

And now you are equipped to recognize and defeat the controlling spirit of Jezebel.

Now we'll look at some of the deeply personal attacks the devil launches, and how God equips us to overcome them.

SECTION FOUR

SATAN'S TACTICS

Satan's attacks can be honed to a sharp point, designed to hit your most tender spot.

25

DO YOU EVER FEEL WORTHLESS?

Let's steal the devil's playbook. Let's see what his plans are for you and me. Sometimes he sends out his generals to advertise sin—like Belial seducing people with sex, alcohol, and disrespect or Jezebel with her lust for power, manipulation and control. Those kinds of attacks are like a billboard—aimed at everyone, but only effective against those who respond.

However, the devil also launches more personal attacks custom-designed to trip you up. These are not just billboards but personalized assaults intended to bring you down where you have a weakness. Satan's attacks can be honed to a sharp point, designed to hit your most tender spot.

I've identified two dozen of the devil's tactics. There are certainly many more, but these particular snares play a big part in his arsenal of personalized weapons. They are like "smart bombs" that drive straight home and do the most damage.

FEELING WORTHLESS.

Have you ever felt that you had lost your value? Maybe you're a mom and your sons and daughters have grown up; they don't rely on you like they used to, and you feel worthless. Maybe you've lost your job, and you feel like you don't have anything valuable to contribute to life anymore. Maybe you've been down in the "doldrums" so long you feel like your existence is pointless.

I have felt worse than worthless. There have been times when people around me seemed to have so much more talent, were so much smarter and more clever than I could ever hope to be. I wondered why anyone bothered to pay attention to me.

Why does the devil use this approach? Because he knows God loves you. If he can make you feel miserable and worthless, he's hurting God's heart. Furthermore, if he can get you to believe you really are worthless, you become worthless.

ROCK-THROWING

The devil employed this tactic on King David.

> **And as David and his men went by the way, Shimei went along on the hill's side over against him, and cursed as he went, and threw stones at him, and cast dust.**
>
> **And the king, and all the people that were with him, came weary….**
>
> —2 Samuel 16:13–14a

This took place when David was in exile, and his son Absalom attempted to take over the kingdom. David found himself in a heap of trouble. You can imagine what was going through his mind. "God gave me this kingdom and now it's being ripped right out from under me. What have I done?" Maybe he felt God was punishing him. He probably felt confused.

Then the devil got personal. He sent along Shimei to further torment him. He wanted to kick David when he was already reeling, so he started a cursing and rock-throwing campaign. That sounds like what the Pharisees did to a woman caught in adultery, doesn't it? It sounds like what the Pharisees did to Stephen. Shimei and the Pharisees possessed the same merciless character—the devil's character.

The enemy will come at you like he came at David. He doesn't necessarily use nuclear bombs. Sometimes he just tosses rocks. Maybe your husband makes a comment, and the devil twists the words before they get to your ear. He has thrown a rock at you, making you feel worthless.

I read about a young altar boy in a church in Europe. He was helping one of the priests serve communion, but accidentally dropped a vial of wine on the altar. The priest slapped him and said, "You worthless boy." That young man bowed his head and walked off the platform. The priest's hasty words made him feel worthless to the priest and to God. He went on to become a communist leader in Yugoslavia. He figured if he was so worthless why not go against God?

REACTIONS TO WORTHLESSNESS

That's one reaction to feeling worthless. Here are some other symptoms you may see or experience when the devil attacks through feelings of worthlessness:

1. People who don't know their worth to God are out of harmony with him.

They can't get in step with his plans.

2. A person who doesn't understand his true worth to God never fully realizes his dreams.

He may have big dreams, but he doesn't initiate a plan of action.

3. Individuals who don't feel valuable are sad and depressed.

They move from place to place hoping a change of scenery or job or church will help them, but it doesn't. They don't realize that they have great value right where they are.

4. They try to run from their problems.
When you run from one problem, you inevitably run right into five more.

5. They bypass exciting opportunities.
Every opportunity includes some risk, but feelings of worthlessness defeat you before you begin.

How can you make your sense of worth grow? Let me share with you six keys to know you're worth something to the Lord.

*Each of us has a mission. If we don't know
what it is, and we aren't working
toward achieving it,
we feel useless.*

26

WORTH SOMETHING TO GOD

You are worth something to God! In fact, as a child of God you are worth more to Him than you can possibly imagine. It may seem impossible, but it's true. Occasionally, it's good to remind yourself of this, and that's the first strategy to help your sense of worth grow.

KNOW WHAT THE BIBLE SAYS ABOUT YOU

I have a big notebook marked, "Believe You Can Do It." I start reading the Bible in Genesis and work all the way through to Revelation looking for Scriptures proving I can do what God has called me to do. Over the years that notebook has grown thicker and thicker. For example, the Bible says:

> **Therefore if any man be in Christ, he is a new creature: old things are passed away; behold, all things are become new.**
> **—2 Corinthians 5:17**

When the devil comes to me and says, "You're a worthless old sinner." I say, "The Bible says I am a new creation. The old is gone and the new has come. Now, devil, get out of here!"

In Psalms there is a beautiful description of man's position in God's plan:

> For thou hast made him a little lower than
> the angels, and hast crowned him with glory and
> honour.
>
> —Psalm 8:5

Why walk around gloomy if God has crowned you with glory and honor?

The Bible says you are a king and priest (Rev. 1:6; 5:10). Would God make a worm into a ruler? Of course not! Even if you were a worm before, now you are a king and priest.

Jesus said:

> Ye are the salt of the earth....
> Ye are the light of the world....
>
> —Matthew 5:13a, 14a

Jesus did not say, "Try your best to be the salt of the earth." He said, "You *are* the salt of the earth. You *are* the light of the world."

Ephesians 2:10 says:

> For we are his workmanship, created in Christ
> Jesus unto good works, which God hath before
> ordained that we should walk in them.

The word "workmanship" in the Greek means you're his masterpiece in the making.

> And the LORD shall make thee the head, and
> not the tail....
>
> —Deuteronomy 28:13a

God called you to be a winner, not a loser!

Start your own file or list of Scriptures that prove your worth. When the devil tries to get you down, reach for it and remind yourself of your value to God.

MORE STRATEGIES
1. List your talents and special abilities.

God gave us all special talents. I'm quite certain you can't think of one person who doesn't have strength in one area or another. It's true of you, too! Only false humility confesses no talent. Paul said to have a sober opinion of yourself, to recognize where you're weak and where you're strong (Romans 12:3). It's good to remind yourself of the special ways God has gifted you.

2. Pray and thank God for who you are in Christ and for your special abilities.

Have you noticed how gratitude flows once it's uncorked? Even if you don't feel worthy, thank God for your immeasurable worth and soon your emotions will start to believe it. Put facts before your feelings, and the feelings will follow.

The way to get that flow of gratitude going is to read the Word and pray. God will give you revelation of how much worth you have.

3. Ask God to reveal your mission in life.

Each of us has a mission. If you don't know what it is, and you aren't working toward achieving it, you feel useless.

Mary Ann was having her coffee break one morning and feeling worthless. "God, what use am I to your Kingdom?" she asked. "Reveal to me what my mission in life is." Then it dawned on her that she could have a Bible study in her home during coffee break and invite the women in the neighborhood to come.

At first she felt embarrassed going door to door, but the first three women were so enthusiastic that it encouraged her to go to her other neighbors. Soon, she had a little neighborhood Bible study meeting regularly in her home. People were being saved. God's Kingdom grew. So many women attended that they had to branch off and start a second Bible study in another neighborhood. It became a prosperous effort for the Lord Jesus Christ; Mary Ann found her mission.

You might do something like that. Ask God to give you an idea for how you can serve his Kingdom, and when you receive God's plan, follow it with all your might.

4. Live a disciplined life.

Inconsistent discipline produces insecurity and leads to self-condemnation and feelings of worthlessness. You might read the Bible for two days and the other five you skip it. That's inconsistent discipline.

When you stick to a routine, no matter if you feel like it or not, you respect yourself more.

5. Realize that your worth doesn't depend on what other people do.

A lot of times I listen for "Amen" when I preach, and I think my sermon is worthless if I don't hear a bunch. Sometimes the sermons I think are the worst—when people sit there without saying anything and nobody pats me on the back afterwards—are the ones that sell out at the audio desk.

You can't look to other people to give you worth. They weren't meant to. Your worth comes from God.

The devil's got nothing on you. When you're reminded of your amazing worth, you can resist the devil. Remember:

- Understand what the Bible says about who you are in Christ.
- Understand your talents and special abilities.
- Look for creative ways of using them.
- Give thanks to God. Pray daily.
- Develop a mission.
- Live a disciplined life.

- Realize that your worth comes from God, not people.

Let the devil throw his rocks. They'll bounce right off you without leaving a scratch!

When your affections are not on heavenly things, you become less useful to God.

27

STOLEN AFFECTIONS?

Another of Satan's battle tactics is to redirect your focus away from God to other things. In Colossians the Bible says:

> **Since you have been raised to new life with Christ, set your sights on the realities of heaven, where Christ sits in the place of honor at God's right hand.**
> **Think about the things of heaven, not the things of earth.**
>
> —Colossians 3:1–2 (NLT)

When your affections are not on heavenly things, you become less useful to God. Your mind becomes paralyzed.

When I first worked in full-time ministry, I didn't make much money. Mary Jo and I were making $125 a week. One day I looked on the kitchen table where we kept our bills. There was a bill for $161.10. I didn't know where we would get the money to pay it. Soon that bill was all I could think about. My mind and affections got off the things of God and on to that bill. For days, my mind was paralyzed and I couldn't even pray properly. My spiritual life was neutralized.

I went in my bedroom and prayed, "Lord, I've tried praying; I've tried praising you; I've tried everything and I don't know why my mind keeps going back to that bill and how I will pay it. I feel like you can't even hear my prayers, much

less answer them. What in the world am I supposed to do?"
Then a Scripture came to me:

> **And the Holy Spirit helps us in our weakness.
> For example, we don't know what God wants us
> to pray for. But the Holy Spirit prays for us with
> groanings that cannot be expressed in words.**
> **—Romans 8:26 (NLT)**

So, I said, "Lord, I'm going to groan. Ugggghhhhh!
Uggggghhhh!"

After awhile I became quiet, and words entered my mind
from my spirit. They were, "Whatsoever you bind on earth
will be bound in Heaven. Whatsoever you loose on earth will
be loosed in Heaven." These words are from Matthew 16:19;
I didn't know what they meant, but I had a good feeling in
my belly. So I prayed, "Lord, I'm not sure what that Scripture
means, but if it means that I can loose angels on earth and
you'll loose them from Heaven to help me out of this mess,
then I loose them." Instantly, the sense of oppression began to
leave. I closed my eyes and saw a picture of demon spirits all
around me trying to hinder my prayers, and as I prayed they
were booted out of the room.

My mind got back on the Word of God, and though that
bill was still there, it didn't steal my affections. Within a few
days, by a miracle of supply, it was paid off in full!

OFF CENTER

If your affections have ever been stolen, rest assured you're
not the first. The first humans fell for this trick of the devil.

> **And the LORD God commanded the man,
> saying, Of every tree of the garden thou mayest
> freely eat:**

> But of the tree of the knowledge of good and
> evil, thou shalt not eat of it: for in the day that
> thou eatest thereof thou shalt surely die.
>
> —Genesis 2:16–17

Things were really going well between God and Adam and Eve. He'd come down in the cool of the day to fellowship with his creation. Can you imagine a knock at your door in the evening, and there stands the Lord? He says, "I thought I'd come in and spend some time with you." Wouldn't that be wonderful? You would take a walk or light a fire in the fireplace and sit around and talk with him. That's what life is like when your affections are on him.

But then it says:

> Now the serpent was more subtil than any beast
> of the field which the LORD God had made. And
> he said unto the woman, Yea, hath God said, Ye
> shall not eat of every tree of the garden?
>
> And the woman said unto the serpent, We may
> eat of the fruit of the trees of the garden:
>
> But of the fruit of the tree which is in the midst
> of the garden, God hath said, Ye shall not eat of it,
> neither shall ye touch it, lest ye die.
>
> And the serpent said unto the woman, Ye shall
> not surely die:
>
> For God doth know that in the day ye eat
> thereof, then your eyes shall be opened, and ye
> shall be as gods, knowing good and evil.
>
> And when the woman saw that the tree was
> good for food, and that it was pleasant to the eyes,
> and a tree to be desired to make one wise, she took
> of the fruit thereof, and did eat, and gave also unto
> her husband with her; and he did eat.
>
> And the eyes of them both were opened....
>
> —Genesis 3:1–7a

How effective is the devil at stealing affections? Well, it was the tool he used to bring misery to the entire human race. To us it seems obvious that Adam and Eve shouldn't have eaten the fruit, but how many of us have fallen for the same kind of trick, only to see—in retrospect—we were duped by the same deception?

The devil is subtle. He doesn't invite you to reject God outright, but he makes a plausible argument as to why it's okay to compromise. He may even seem very spiritual as he entices you to forsake simple faith in Jesus and trust your affections to false teachings. Many Bible scholars think the serpent who came to Eve was a flying serpent, as spoken about in Isaiah 14:29. Perhaps Eve mistakenly imagined it was a messenger from the spiritual world.

There are plenty of flying serpents today. They come as so-called messengers from Heaven, and they're not always easy to detect. When you're around people who are being led astray by false teaching, you'll know something is wrong, but you might not be able to put your finger on it. That's what "subtle" means.

ERROR IN THE MIX

Once the members of a Christian church prayed that God would send a professional man to help out in the church. One day, a man walked in and said, "My name is Dr. 'Smith.' I'd like to join the church and help out." The people responded, "Praise the Lord! We prayed someone like you would come." The doctor said all the right things, he seemed like the answer to prayer, but the pastor felt something was not quite right about this new member. He just couldn't pin it down. He thought, "Maybe I'm thinking the worst and not being fair. I'll give him a chance."

The doctor started bringing more and more of his friends to church. Then the whole congregation started feeling weird around the newcomers. One night they prayed, "Lord, what's wrong? They're saying all the right things. They seem to be just who we need." A prophecy came forth from the Lord saying they were wolves in sheep's clothing.

So, they sent delegates to question the new members and found that they were following a man from Korea who claimed to be Christ. The pastor and church members kicked them out and warned other churches about them. The infiltrators screamed, "That's not love. You're supposed to love us!" The pastor answered, "Love without obedience to God's Word is nothing."

You can believe the church had the best prayer meeting ever when they finally got rid of those false prophets!

As you can see, the enemy will subtly try to get you off course. What are the specific ways he'll attempt to steal your simple devotion and get you to put your affections elsewhere? Let's take a look.

Why did Satan deny the death penalty for sin? Because removing the penalty removes the need for a Savior.

28

REFOCUSING YOUR AFFECTIONS

How do we recognize Satan's winged serpents when they come? I see five stages in the devil's plan of attack.

1. He casts doubt on what God has said.

> **And he said unto the woman, Yea, hath God said, ye shall not eat of every tree of the garden?**
> **—Genesis 3:1b**

Why did he ask this question? Bible scholars propose two possibilities: Either he used the ploy to strike up a conversation with Eve and get her talking to him, or he may not have known what God commanded and was probing to see if Eve would tell him and reveal a weakness he could use against her. Eve didn't discern his motive because he was subtle and seemingly spiritual.

2. He denies God's Word outright.

> **And the serpent said unto the woman, ye shall not surely die.**
> **—Genesis 3:4**

The Bible is clear—the wage of sin is death (Romans 6:23), but Satan denied that fact. I remember Bishop Pike, a minister who was led to doubt the virgin birth of Jesus Christ because he couldn't understand, with his natural mind, how a child could be born of a virgin. Satan then took him to the second stage, deception, and taught Pike how to become a "medium" and have conversations with spirits from another world. Finally, Pike went on national television and denied the Word of God.

Many people still fall for the lie that sin won't lead to death, though the Bible clearly states it will. The Bible says:

> Know ye not that the unrighteous shall not inherit the kingdom of God? Be not deceived: neither fornicators, nor idolaters, nor adulterers, nor effeminate, nor abusers of themselves with mankind,
>
> Nor thieves, nor covetous, nor drunkards, nor revilers, nor extortioners, shall inherit the kingdom of God.
>
> —1 Corinthians 6:9–10

Why did Satan deny the death penalty for sin? Because removing the penalty removes the need for a Savior.

FALSE IMPROVEMENTS

3. He promises great rewards for disobedience.

Satan promised Eve great improvement if she would disobey God's law. He implied, "If you listen to me, your eyes will be opened. You're kind of a dimwit now. God wants to keep something good from you, but if you listen to me you'll rise up to the level of God."

New Christians—in misplaced zeal for spiritual things—sometimes run to different teachings that claim "new" revelation and "deeper" meaning. If they're not careful, they will find delusion instead of revelation.

John Alexander Dowie was a great man of God in the late 19th and early 20th centuries. He became one of the great proponents of divine healing, and many were healed and delivered through his ministry. He was also the founder of the city of Zion, Illinois. He got so caught up in building the city that his prayer life allegedly tapered off.

One day, a man told him he'd had a revelation from God that Dowie was actually the prophesied Elijah who the Bible says will come back before the return of Jesus. Initially Dowie rejected the idea, but slowly, step-by-step, he came to believe it. One day he announced that he was indeed Elijah.

He abandoned simple faith in Jesus and it ruined his ministry. Ultimately, he died a penniless, friendless man deserted by his family and plagued by accusations and scandal.

How does Jesus feel when we set our affections elsewhere? Think of the story of the sailor who came home from the war a month earlier than expected. When he knocked on the door, another man answered wearing the sailor's own clothes. The sailor's wife's voice rang out from the back, "Honey, who is it?" Imagine how heartbroken her husband must have felt as he said, "Never mind, I must have the wrong house." That's probably how Jesus feels when we embrace someone else's false philosophies—betrayed and heartbroken.

SUPER-POWERS

4. He promises elevation to "god" status.

Satan promised Eve "god" status if she ate the forbidden fruit. Everyone would love to have super-powers. One cult says you may become a god of your own planet after death. This idea attracts people because the heart of sin wants to claim all worship for itself. That is Satan's desire, and so he preys on man's ambition to become greater than God created him to be.

5. He implies God is selfish and controlling.

The final step was implying God did not have man's best interests in mind when he made the rule. Satan implied God was jealously guarding this "knowledge of good and evil," and didn't want them to become "as gods." Don't ever forget man is made lower than God. Adam and Eve were not "co-gods" with God. Jesus is the only one equal to God. He is the Head; we are the body. But Satan implied God was keeping Adam and Eve from their rightful place. He cast doubt over God's trustworthiness. He made God look like the bad guy, and Eve fell for it.

Today, people still fall for these same tactics. They are deluded into thinking they can program their own spiritual destinies, instead of simply trusting God and his revealed Word. No successful relationship with God can be based on distrust of his motives.

These five steps lead people away from simple faith in Christ. The good news is found in a prophecy God gave:

> **And the LORD God said unto the serpent,**
> **Because thou hast done this, thou art cursed above**
> **all cattle, and above every beast of the field; upon**
> **thy belly shalt thou go, and dust shalt thou eat all**
> **the days of thy life:**
> **And I will put enmity between thee and the**
> **woman, and between thy seed and her seed; it shall**
> **bruise thy head, and thou shalt bruise his heel.**
> **—Genesis 3:14–15**

The dictionary defines sophistry as subtle, tricky, super-ficially believable but false methods of reasoning. Those are the arguments Satan uses, but you don't have to fall for them. You don't have to submit to his lures to draw you away from simple devotion to Jesus. Stay on the winning side. Listen to the Holy Spirit when winged serpents insinuate that God doesn't have your best in mind. Keep your faith simple and straightforward, like the Gospel we believe in. Then your affections will be pure.

Next we'll see how the devil sharpens his claws when we become weary.

When you're weak and weary your
mind doesn't hold together well,
and thoughts slip through
you would routinely
turn away.

29

WHEN YOU'RE WEAK AND WEARY

During the Korean War, the enemy captured a U.S. ship. The commander and his crew were put in a miserable prison camp where the enemy used every possible tactic to exhaust them. They made them stay awake for days without sleep and beat on the bars if they nodded off. The commander was under so much strain that he succumbed to the temptation to attempt suicide. He was unsuccessful, but tormenting thoughts continually bombarded his mind: "You've lost a U.S. ship and its top secret records. You'll go down in disgrace. You'll probably lose your rank." He was so weak and weary he believed it.

But when he eventually returned to the U.S., he was hailed as a hero, a courageous man who endured prison. The reality was exactly the opposite of what he expected.

AN OPPORTUNE TIME

The devil comes after us whenever he can, but his greatest successes come when we're weak and weary.

> Moreover Ahithophel said unto Absalom, Let me now choose out twelve thousand men, and I will arise and pursue after David this night:
> And I will come upon him while he is weary and weak handed, and will make him afraid: and

> all the people that are with him shall flee; and I
> will smite the king only.
>
> —2 Samuel 17:1–2

David's son Absalom, following personal ambition, wanted to overthrow his father's kingdom. He won the hearts of many people in Israel and some of David's top advisors. Absalom was not anointed by God to be king, and his government was founded on deception.

One of those traitorous advisors was Ahithophel. A quick character study of David and Ahithophel shows David was motivated by God, and the other by the devil.

David's name in the Hebrew means "beloved." He was faithful in the small things, even as a boy tending a little flock of sheep. Later he slew a giant who was persecuting God's people. He organized genuine worship of God in Israel and made the plans for the building of the temple. He wrote seventy-three psalms, many of which are still sung today. He expanded the kingdom of Israel in every direction, and the Bible says he was a man after God's own heart. David wasn't perfect, but he was motivated by God.

Ahithophel's name in Hebrew means "brother of folly." He was driven by ambition for personal power. He counseled Absalom to commit adultery, and eventually Ahithophel himself committed suicide. Who else in the Bible committed suicide? Judas Iscariot. Who does the Bible say possessed Judas? The devil. Who else committed suicide? Saul. What motivated him? An evil spirit. Suicide has the devil's fingerprints all over it.

Ahithophel said, "I will make him afraid." Of course, God has not given us a spirit of fear, but of love, and of power and a sound mind (2 Timothy 1:7). Who gives a spirit of fear and cringing? The devil. Then Ahithophel promised to smite the king—characteristic of the murderous devil—and he promised peace if his advice was followed. The devil always makes false promises of peace. In fact, the Antichrist himself will appear to bring peace to the world (1 Thessalonians 5:3), but in fact he will bring destruction.

VULNERABLE

Ahithophel recognized that David was weak, weary, and vulnerable to attack. Have you ever felt vulnerable? Jesus knew that feeling when He fasted for forty days in the wilderness and the devil tempted Him (Matthew 4). After the first few days of fasting the hunger leaves and you feel a surge of strength, but after a few weeks the hunger returns—a sign that you've begun to starve. Jesus had reached the point of starvation and was at his weakest when Satan said, "Tell these stones to become bread" (Matthew 4:3b).

The devil chose the most vulnerable time to attack.

Have you been there? When you're weak and weary your mind doesn't hold together well, and thoughts slip through you would routinely turn away. You begin to doubt your own ability to make right choices.

David Wilkerson was the pastor of a little church in Pennsylvania when he went to New York and started working on the streets. He founded Teen Challenge, worked sixteen hours a day, and was away from home for weeks at a time. He was growing weary but didn't realize it because he loved his work. One day, he was playing with his daughter and a strong urge came over him to throw her down on the floor. Of course he didn't do it, but the urge was there, compelling him. The enemy attacked when he was weak and weary.

Nicky Cruz is another example. He was the head of a street gang in New York before making Jesus the Lord of his life. God changed him and gave him a beautiful wife named

203

Gloria. One morning, very early, Nicky woke up and there was a strange presence in the room with him. He looked at Gloria as the moon shone through the window, and a powerful suggestion spoke in his mind, "Choke her!" The urge was so strong that he almost had his hands around her neck, but instead he woke her up and said,

"Gloria, you've got to get up and pray with me!"

She said, "I'm tired. Don't bother me."

He said, "Honey, I need you now like I've never needed you before. Please get up." They prayed for forty-five minutes; she laid her gentle hands on his head and it was like the Holy Spirit flowed through him and gave him victory over this vile impulse.

It happened to him again on another night and, once more, they got up and prayed. The Lord told him, "Nicky, you've been fasting too much. You've been overworking." All his work made him feel weak and weary.

Some Preacher You Are!

David Yonggi Cho, the pastor of Yoido Full Gospel Church in Seoul, South Korea, the largest church in the world, went through a time when he thought nobody could baptize or serve communion or pray for the sick but him. One day he was at home, weak and weary from financial problems in the family, and his little son came up and said, "Daddy, I'm hungry. Can I have some food?" Cho said, "I don't have any. We'll have to wait until next Sunday and see if the offering is enough that we can buy food." The boy started crying and said, "But Daddy, I'm hungry now!" Cho hauled off and hit the boy. His wife accused, "Some preacher you are. You hit your son." He replied, "Oh, shut up," and hit her, too. Blood streamed down her face. His son was lying on the floor; he thought he had killed him. His wife was screaming at him.

He climbed a tower and went to a window and a voice inside him said, "Jump! Your ministry is ruined anyway. You've hit your son. You're going to be known all over the world as a wife beater. Jump!" He climbed onto the windowsill, and the thought came to him, "Lord, if people who commit suicide don't go to Heaven, let me be the exception."

But another voice inside spoke to him gently and said, "You're the top Pentecostal preacher in South Korea. You're one of the top pastors in the world; if you jump you're going to inspire a lot of people to do the same thing." Cho gathered his wits, went downstairs, asked forgiveness of his wife and son and resumed his ministry. But he learned an important lesson about allowing himself to become so weak and weary that the devil gets a wide-open playing field in which to launch an attack.

How do you recognize that you're weak and weary? I'll give you the warning signs in the next chapter.

It's possible to grow weary in doing good things as quickly as in doing any other activity.

30

WARNING SIGNS OF WEARINESS

The first indicator that you're getting weak and weary is your mind freezes up. You can't seem to think straight. You're dazed and confused.

Then you begin to feel there are more things to do than you have time for. You've got this compelling urge to get things done, but you can't imagine how you will ever do it. You feel your shoulders tighten with tension.

Then you feel like running away from everything, or death might start sounding more attractive all the time.

I'll never forget sitting in my living room feeling like I wasn't doing nearly enough for the Lord. I was working sixteen hours a day but felt I wasn't accomplishing anything. I pictured myself going out to the airport and catching an airplane to anywhere. I just wanted to get away.

Elijah overdid it. He had done a mighty work for God, but now he was physically exhausted. He had cared for the spiritual needs of Israel but neglected his own rest, and eventually he ran into the wilderness to get away (1 Kings 19). The Bible says:

> **And let us not be weary in well doing: for in due season we shall reap, if we faint not.**
> **—Galatians 6:9**

It's possible to grow weary in doing good things as quickly as in doing any other activity.

ANSWERS TO THE PROBLEM

If you find yourself panicking, feeling like you want to die, or run away, because you have so much to do, here are some ideas on getting back on track.

1. Get away and take a rest.

Don't remain in the same environment, under the same stresses, all the time. Jesus set a good example when he took the disciples away to eat and relax (Mark 6:31).

Once, I was at church at 11:30 at night, seeking God's guidance for the next morning's service. My thoughts were scattered. I couldn't seem to focus on anything. I said, "Lord, what's wrong? How come this sermon isn't jelling? Why don't I feel your anointing?" I felt the Lord impress me, "You've been around here too much. Go get a good night's sleep and come back. You'll be refreshed." I did, and the next morning as I was shaving, six sermon points came to me for the service. It's amazing what a little rest and relaxation will accomplish!

When we don't relax, it's a form of pride. We're trying to do more than God has called us to do. We're not resting in the finished work Jesus did at Calvary.

Many years ago my little brother tried to "finish" a guitar I bought in the Philippines. I brought it home and went back overseas. While I was gone, he started sanding it down and sanded a hole right through it! The guitar was already finished, but he tried to "finish" a finished work.

If you've got to keep working, then also work at entering into God's rest. Even God rested (Genesis 2:2–3). Try taking a daily mini-vacation, even if it's for fifteen minutes. Get away from the office, or go to a different part of your office building or job site. The Bible tells us who labor to enter into the rest that God has for us.

> There remaineth therefore a rest to the people of God.
> For he that is entered into his rest, he also hath ceased from his own works, as God did from his.
> Let us labour therefore to enter into that rest, lest any man fall after the same example of unbelief.
>
> —Hebrews 4: 9–11

BEATING WEAKNESS
2. Learn to relax more in everyday life.

> LORD, my heart is not haughty, nor mine eyes lofty: neither do I exercise myself in great matters, or in things too high for me.
>
> —Psalm 131:1

When faced with big things that you can't understand, don't try to figure them out. Say with the psalmist:

> Surely I have behaved and quieted myself, as a child that is weaned of his mother: my soul is even as a weaned child.
> Let Israel hope in the LORD from henceforth and for ever.
>
> —Psalm 131: 2–3

Sometimes we need to get quiet before the Lord. Learn to relax in the midst of life. It doesn't come naturally. In quietness and confidence is your strength, and you receive better guidance when you relax. Even as you work hard, you can be free of strain when you remember that God sees the big picture and knows the answers to the problems and questions that are too big for you to handle.

209

3. Learn to laugh.

A merry heart doeth good like a medicine: but a broken spirit drieth the bones.

—Proverbs 17:22

There was a book called *He Who Laughs Lasts and Lasts and Lasts.* If you want to last, learn the secret of laughing. Learn to wear a smile. Studies continue to show that relaxation and lightheartedness have amazing medical benefits.

4. Learn to pray in the Spirit.

There's nothing more refreshing than speaking in that unknown prayer language God gives (1 Corinthians 14:1–2). I remember getting up feeling tense one Saturday morning because I had to work on my message for Sunday. Finally I said, "I'm going to get quiet and see what the Lord's got." I started walking around my basement, praying in the Spirit. Twenty minutes went by, thirty minutes, thirty-five minutes, and that load on my back began to lift. I got my message for Sunday that day by praying in the Spirit in an unknown language.

5. Most importantly, look to Jesus.

Come unto me, all ye that labour and are heavy laden, and I will give you rest.

—Matthew 11:28

Maybe you're weak and weary; you've been trying to gain favor in God's sight. You've been laboring. Assess yourself; have you been overworking? Maybe you should turn down that extra project or that offer to work overtime. Protect yourself from attack by relaxing, staying strong, getting away from your normal environment, laughing, praying in the Spirit, and focusing on Jesus. It'll make a world of difference—and help you thwart the devil's plans.

The devil's goal is to make you waver in your faith and your decision-making, because the wavering man is of two minds and can't receive anything from the Lord.

31

WHEN EVERYTHING
SEEMS WRONG

Have you ever felt that no matter what you did or said, it was wrong? Have you been in a difficult situation and felt like any decision you made would result in disaster?

One of the devil's chief tactics is to make you think that no matter what you decide, you will be wrong. When the devil worked through the Pharisees, he tried to make Jesus feel like any move He made was wrong. Jesus said of the Pharisees:

But whereunto shall I liken this generation? It is like unto children sitting in the markets, and calling unto their fellows,

And saying, We have piped unto you, and ye have not danced; we have mourned unto you, and ye have not lamented.

For John came neither eating nor drinking, and they say, He hath a devil.

The Son of man came eating and drinking, and they say, Behold a man gluttonous, and a winebibber, a friend of publicans and sinners. But wisdom is justified of her children.

—Matthew 11:16–19

John the Baptist and Jesus had very different styles. John was so out of sync with popular culture that he wore an old camel hair coat. He didn't socialize with people and didn't preach from a fancy pulpit in a beautiful church facility. He went into the wilderness and people still came to him. He preached, "Repent, for the kingdom of Heaven is near" (Matthew 3:2).

How did the Pharisees respond? They said he was demon possessed!

Then along came Jesus whose earthly ministry style was the opposite of John's. He rubbed shoulders with sinners, talked to Samaritan women, and went to weddings and receptions. So, the Pharisees said he was a gluttonous man, an alcoholic, and later they accused him of being demon possessed. In other words, you're wrong no matter what you do!

The devil loves to make people feel that they're wrong no matter what. Every decision you make will have supporters and opponents, and it's important to grasp that it's not wrong for people to misunderstand or disagree with you, but it's wrong to let those misunderstandings eat at you so that you feel cornered.

WHICH WAY?

There are times when decisions must be made in the midst of uncertainty. King David was faced with a decision when he found out Absalom had overthrown his kingdom. Should he stay and fight and take a chance on innocent blood being shed, or should he flee the palace? David instantly made a decision based on what he felt was the right thing to do. He gathered his men and fled the castle, and in the end God honored that decision (2 Samuel 15).

The late Quinton Edwards of Cypress Cathedral in Florida was faced with a decision when Cypress Cathedral was being built. He wasn't the type to ask people for money. He believed that when God guides, God provides, but he came to a point where their funds were completely drained. All the money had gone into construction.

He had to decide: should he share the need with the congregation and run the risk of people thinking he was just scamming them for money, or should he keep quiet and wait on God to meet the need? If the money didn't come in, the construction people were going to stop work and it would cost twice as much to get the crew back. It seemed that no matter what he did, it would be the wrong decision.

Edwards decided to tell the people about the need. He got in the pulpit and said, "I don't want to sound like I'm begging for money, but we're faced with an urgent need. The construction of the cathedral is going to stop if we don't meet this need. I'm not saying I want you to give, but pray that God will supply the need. We've got to have it by tomorrow morning."

That Sunday night, the offering was enough to keep the construction going. Today the church is completed and ministering to people's needs.

WAVERING

The devil's goal is to make you waver in your faith and your decision making, because the wavering man is of two minds and can't receive anything from the Lord.

> If any of you lack wisdom, let him ask of God, that giveth to all men liberally, and upbraideth not; and it shall be given him.
> But let him ask in faith, nothing wavering. For he that wavereth is like a wave of the sea driven with the wind and tossed.
> For let not that man think that he shall receive any thing of the Lord.

> **A double minded man is unstable in all his ways.**
>
> —James 1:5-8

The devil wants unstable Christians running around the earth. Without faith you can't please God, and if your faith is wavering it's not going to please God.

How many times have you made a decision only to hear a little voice say, "You're wrong!"? So you move in another direction and hear, "You're wrong!" You end up going back and forth, never getting anywhere.

Often we're faced with decisions that don't seem to offer a right way. Jesus was in many situations like that. Next time you read the Gospels, notice how many times the Pharisees tried to put Him in a no-win situation.

How do you find the counsel of God in decision making? I've found a few keys to making decisions and knowing that the wisdom is from God.

Decisions are almost always based on one of two kinds of wisdom: false wisdom, which is devilish, or true wisdom, which is from above.

32

HOW TO KNOW YOU'RE RIGHT

The reason I'm in full-time ministry is because of these verses:

> If any of you lack wisdom, let him ask of God, that giveth to all men liberally, and upbraideth not; and it shall be given him.
> But let him ask in faith, nothing wavering. For he that wavereth is like a wave of the sea driven with the wind and tossed.
> For let not that man think that he shall receive any thing of the Lord.
> A double minded man is unstable in all his ways.
>
> — James 1:5–8

I was at a point of decision and didn't know which way to turn, so I sat in my living room one day and asked God what to do, and He told me. It was that simple. But I learned about the process of decision making and here's the advice I offer when you face a tough choice.

1. Get all the facts you can.

Try to get as much knowledge as you possibly can. If you want to build a house in a particular area, find out if it ever floods there. Check out the local schools. Ask about the neighborhood. Do everything you can so that your ignorance doesn't lead you into a bad decision.

2. Ask God for special wisdom.

Jeremiah 33:3 says, "Call unto me, and I will answer you." It doesn't say, "I might answer you if I feel like it." And James, chapter one, says if you need wisdom just ask. Get down on your knees and ask for help!

3. Listen for God's answer.

Your answer may come through a Heaven-sent idea, a Scripture, a Christian friend, a television program, a radio program, a conversation, a magazine, or a Sunday morning sermon—but your answer will come, guaranteed.

4. Move ahead unswervingly.

In Proverbs the Bible says:

> **Commit thy works unto the LORD, and thy thoughts shall be established.**
> **—Proverbs 16:3**

When you are faced with a decision, the biggest compliment God can give you is to trust you to make the decision based on your knowledge of him. He'll give you wisdom, but it won't be something you see or hear. It will be something on the inside causing you to make the right decision. It means you've matured to the point where God can trust you to make a decision based on his character and will. It means you know God really well, even if you don't always feel like you do.

Commit your decision to the Lord, and God guarantees it'll be successful. If it was the wrong decision for some reason, God is able to correct your course gently and lovingly.

WISDOM FROM ABOVE?

How do you detect if wisdom is from above or if it's from Satan? The Bible tells us there are different kinds of wisdom.

> Who is a wise man and endued with knowledge
> among you? let him shew out of a good conversa-
> tion his works with meekness of wisdom.
> But if ye have bitter envying and strife in your
> hearts, glory not, and lie not against the truth.
> This wisdom descendeth not from above, but is
> earthly, sensual, devilish.
> For where envying and strife is, there is confu-
> sion and every evil work.
>
> —James 3:13–16

Decisions are almost always based on one of two kinds of wisdom: false wisdom, which is devilish, or true wisdom, which is from above. False wisdom produces decisions that the devil delights in. It springs from:

- **Bitter envy**
  This is when you make a decision out of jealousy.
  Perhaps you want a new house or car because the
  neighbors got one.
- **Selfish ambition**
  Or as the King James Version says, "strife in your
  hearts." That's a decision designed to get you to the
  top, no matter whom you have to step on.
- **An earthly perspective**
  This means it only takes this world into account.
  When you were born again, you entered into a
  different kingdom. Eons from now we will be alive,
  so, it's important to make our present decisions with
  the next world in mind. Don't be like Esau, who
  sold his birthright for a bowl of beans (Genesis 25),
  or like Judas, who betrayed the Lord for thirty pieces
  of silver.

- **Sensuality**
  Devilish wisdom is based on what you can see, hear, taste, touch, and smell. It discounts anything outside the five senses.

HOW DO WE DETECT TRUE WISDOM?

- **It's pure.**
  God's wisdom has no ulterior motives. It's clean and pure. It produces right relationships and is gentle and considerate of others. When you make a decision, decide what is going to benefit the greatest number of people involved.
- **It's not stubborn.**
  There's a divine reasonableness about Heaven-sent wisdom. It's full of mercy and good fruit. It isn't defensive or insecure. It considers all sides.
- **It's wholehearted.**
  True wisdom goes all out. It dives in with passion and enthusiasm. It launches out into the deep. It isn't lukewarm and doesn't vacillate or waiver.
- **It's without hypocrisy.**
  True wisdom is sincere and honest. It doesn't disguise its real motives.

At times we all have felt—no matter what decision we make—it will be wrong. Don't let the devil mix you up! Look at the situation and gather all the knowledge you can. Say, "Father, grant me wisdom from above." It will come. Test it to make sure it's from God. Then move straight ahead, and don't be dissuaded. That's how to find the counsel of God when making decisions—and thereby avoid the traps of the devil.

God promised no weapon formed against you will prosper. So, don't fear mockery.

33

HANDLING RIDICULE

We've seen how the enemy tries to make us feel worthless, tries to take our eyes and affections off Jesus Christ, strikes when we're weak and weary, and tries to make us feel wrong no matter what we do. He might also try a fifth tactic: ridicule.

In John 9, Jesus had just performed a creative miracle on a man born blind. Jesus picked up some dirt, spit in it, rolled it into a ball, placed the mud ball on the man's eye socket, and told him to wash in the pool of Siloam. But when the religious leaders heard about this, they ridiculed the man.

> Then said they to him again, What did he to thee? how opened he thine eyes?
>
> He answered them, I have told you already, and ye did not hear: wherefore would ye hear it again? will ye also be his disciples?
>
> Then they reviled him, and said, Thou art his disciple; but we are Moses' disciples.
>
> We know that God spake unto Moses: as for this fellow, we know not from whence he is....
>
> They answered and said unto him, Thou wast altogether born in sins, and dost thou teach us? And they cast him out.
>
> —John 9:26–29, 34

Imagine that! This man spent years in darkness until Jesus healed him, and the religious leaders ridiculed him and threw him out of the synagogue!

This is one of Satan's principle tactics. After you receive a legitimate experience from the Lord, Satan will immediately send along somebody to ridicule you, to try and reverse the change God made in your life. When Jesus was baptized in the Jordan, the Holy Spirit drove Him into the wilderness where the devil ridiculed Him. God said,

> And a voice from heaven said, "This is my Son, whom I love; with him I am well pleased."
> —Matthew 3:17 (TNIV)

Satan countered with,

> "If you are the Son of God," he said, "throw yourself down. For it is written:
> " 'He will command his angels concerning you, and they will lift you up in their hands, so that you will not strike your foot against a stone.' "
> —Matthew 4:6 (TNIV)

It also happened to the disciples after the Resurrection:

> And suddenly there came a sound from heaven as of a rushing mighty wind, and it filled all the house where they were sitting.
> And there appeared unto them cloven tongues like as of fire, and it sat upon each of them.
> And they were all filled with the Holy Ghost, and began to speak with other tongues, as the Spirit gave them utterance.
> And there were dwelling at Jerusalem Jews, devout men, out of every nation under heaven.
> Now when this was noised abroad, the multitude came together, and were confounded, be-

cause that every man heard them speak in his own
language....
And they were all amazed, and were in doubt,
saying one to another, What meaneth this?
Others mocking said, These men are full of
new wine.

—Acts 2:2–6, 12–13

In the midst of the most wonderful experience imagin-
able, the devil sent men to ridicule and call them drunkards!

BUS BIBLE STUDY

Once, I was on a Greyhound bus, and I began speaking
with the person sitting next to me about spiritual matters.
Then the people in front, behind, and across the aisle from us
joined the discussion until we had a whole Bible study going on! I handed out pamphlets by Oral Roberts about how
to receive the baptism in the Holy Spirit, and people were
sincerely interested.

Then a woman from the back of the bus came up,
snatched one of my pamphlets and said, "You're really sick.
You don't know your head from a hole in the ground. This
is nonsense. You ought to read a book by so-and-so. He'd
set you straight." I almost dissolved in my chair. Everybody
turned back to his or her seat. I thought her outburst had ruined everything, but then I invited those people to my house,
and that night a whole houseful of people got filled with the
Holy Spirit! We were in my living room until two o'clock in
the morning.

Another time, I was a pump operator at the power com-
pany, and I returned from a healing and miracle service and
word got around that I had some amazing stories to tell. I
had seen blind eyes opened, people in wheel chairs get up and
walk. I shared the great things God was doing, but the devil

was around the corner looking for a way to ridicule me. The foreman, a 65-year old professing Christian, came down to my desk all bent over and acting like he'd been injured. He said, "Oh, heal me!" and jumped up straight, mocking me. It felt terrible that a fellow believer would mock me.

Instead of withdrawing I decided to pray for him. I knew that a man of his age couldn't handle losing sleep, so at one a.m. I got up and prayed, "Lord, please wake him up and convict him of his ridicule and draw him to yourself." I peeked out the front window looking across the park to where he lived, and the lights in his house went on. I thought, "Thank you, Lord; you are at work!"

The next morning, I was working in the water chemical treatment plant and this man came in. This time he really was hunched over. His hair was messed up, and he was rubbing his eyes. I asked, "What's the matter? Looks like you didn't get enough sleep last night."

He said, "I slept good."

I replied, "I did see your light on over there about 1:30." He turned and walked away, but later that day he told me, "I felt terrible all night long. I want to apologize to you. I don't want to be in trouble with God. What you're doing is good."

Yes, you may be ridiculed up front, but later you'll see fruit even from people who mocked you!

TURN RIDICULE INTO BLESSING

The prophets Elijah and Elisha were often ridiculed after they made great prophetic announcements (1 Kings 19; 2 Kings 2). His own wife mocked King David, and God struck her barren (2 Samuel 6). Jesus went to heal a little girl and was laughed at.

> And when he was come in, he saith unto them,
> Why make ye this ado, and weep? the damsel is not
> dead, but sleepeth.
> And they laughed him to scorn.
>
> —Mark 5:39–40a

It happens to all God's people. Let's see three ways you can turn ridicule into something good.

1. Don't fear ridicule. Jesus said:

> Woe unto you, when all men shall speak well
> of you!
>
> —Luke 6:26a

Ridicule will come, but ask yourself, "Is this ridicule or criticism deserved?" If it is, make some adjustments in your life. But if it's not, don't fear it. Isaiah says:

> No weapon that is formed against thee shall
> prosper; and every tongue that shall rise against
> thee in judgment thou shalt condemn. This is the
> heritage of the servants of the LORD, and their
> righteousness is of me, saith the LORD.
>
> —Isaiah 54:17

Maybe you're a businessman and other businessmen are ridiculing you for standing up for Christian principles. Maybe you're a student in high school being ridiculed for your faith. Maybe you're the only believing wife and mother on the block and the rest of the women gossip about you all the time.

God promised no weapon formed against you will prosper. So, don't fear mockery.

2. Pray for those who ridicule you.

They are Satan's tool and are lost unless somebody intercedes for them. It is written (1 Corinthians 6:10) that abusive people have no place in the Kingdom of Heaven. You might be the only person who will pray for their salvation.

3. Bless those who ridicule you. Paul says:

> ...being reviled, we bless; being persecuted, we suffer it....
> —1 Corinthians 4:12b

Pray that the Lord will keep them up all night and convict them. That's returning good for evil!

Facing ridicule is the price you pay on the road to great achievements. Dream big, think big, pray big, believe big, make big faith promises—and know there will be mockers on the sidelines. That is their problem. Don't fear them or their abusive words. Pray for your mockers, bless those who curse you, and turn what the devil meant for harm into a tool to build God's Kingdom.

The only question we need to ask about any situation is, "What is the will of God?" concerning the matter.

34

MORE TERRIBLE TACTICS

I read a book about a famous Christian pianist written by an author who made him out to be a terrible man. When I finished I couldn't help thinking what a rotten guy he was because there were so many serious allegations against him. I could hardly believe he was a minister of the Gospel. Soon after the book was released, he stopped getting invitations to minister, but a year later the truth came out—the author sensationalized and fabricated the whole story. There were half-truths, misrepresentations, and outright lies. This pianist was a true minister of God, but a brother in Christ betrayed him.

Chances are you have been betrayed, especially if you're a strong believer. The devil's nature is betrayal (think of Judas Iscariot or Ahithophel). The Bible says in the last days family members will betray each other.

> This know also, that in the last days perilous times shall come.
> For men shall be lovers of their own selves, covetous, boasters, proud, blasphemers, disobedient to parents, unthankful, unholy,
> Without natural affection, trucebreakers, false accusers, incontinent, fierce, despisers of those that are good,

Traitors, heady, highminded, lovers of pleasures
more than lovers of God;
Having a form of godliness, but denying the
power thereof: from such turn away.
—2 Timothy 3:1–5

You've probably felt the sting of someone turning on you, playing the Benedict Arnold. One of the communists' tactics during the height of the Soviet Union's power was for teachers to keep an eye out for religious kids. They were to befriend them and undermine their family relationships so the kids would turn in their parents as enemies of the state.

What do you do when someone betrays you? Bless them. Return good for evil. You don't have to continue the friendship, but, as far as it's possible, live at peace with them. Remember, God has never and will never betray you.

BIRDS OF A FEATHER

Another enemy tactic is to get you to follow the wrong crowd and be a crowd pleaser. Pilate was a crowd pleaser. He found no fault in Jesus, but the crowds shouted, "Crucify him!" Against his own conscience, Pilate turned Jesus over to be crucified (Matthew 27).

When I was having problems in the church, a wise man told me, "You worry too much about what other people think." He was right. When I've been at my lowest and felt the worst, I was worried about what other people were thinking instead of what Jesus was thinking.

The only question we need to ask about any situation is, "What is the will of God?" concerning the matter. Then move ahead with his will and people will get in line. God will make a successful way for you. He is the "Way Maker!"

A young girl named Virginia was in her church's Easter play and had practice on Sunday afternoons. One Friday, some of her girlfriends invited her to go to a weekend party. Virginia declined, and they ridiculed her for being "goody-goody." But on Sunday morning, those girls walked into her church, each wearing a disgruntled look on their faces. Virginia asked, "What are you doing here?" They replied, "We felt guilty so we came to check out your church." They were the first ones to receive Christ at the altar that Sunday because they were impressed when Virginia stood firm for what she believed instead of being a crowd pleaser.

WHICH STATE ARE YOU IN?

Another tactic of the devil is to try to keep you in a constant state of fear. He'll tell you you've got cancer or heart problems. He'll tell you God's Word doesn't work, that it's outdated. Some "theologian" will say that the power of God died with the apostles. Satan will try anything to stir up fear.

Of course, none of his lies are true. Fear is the reverse of faith. Faith pleases God and gets results. What's the antidote to fear? Faith!

> **So then faith cometh by hearing, and hearing by the word of God.**
> —Romans 10:17

BAD BUSINESS

The devil will lie about your ministry or business. That's what Elymas did to Paul and Barnabas (Acts 13). It's what the religious leaders did to Jesus and his Apostles. How many times have you heard lies or rumors about a ministry or prominent Christian who got a lot of bad press, but in the end the lies and rumors weren't true? That's the devil at work.

In 1978 rumors were going around that Oral Roberts had an abundance of money and didn't need any more. People quit sending offerings to him when he needed them the most. An important building project was endangered because someone spread lies.

If you hear stories circulating, find their source and then speak against them by telling the truth. Don't give lies any foothold. In the end, truth will stand strong and lies will crumble to the ground.

HE'LL SAY YOU'RE GREAT

If he can't discourage you, the devil will go the other way and tell you that you're God's gift to planet Earth. He tried to do that to Paul and Barnabas in Acts 14. The Bible says:

> **And when the people saw what Paul had done, they lifted up their voices, saying in the speech of Lycaonia, The gods are come down to us in the likeness of men.**
> **And they called Barnabas, Jupiter; and Paul, Mercurius, because he was the chief speaker.**
> **—Acts 14:11–12**

It would have been tempting for Paul and Barnabas to say, "Hey, we must be pretty great! We'll have our own chariot. They'll provide a mansion for us, and we'll have servants for the rest of our lives." Instead, they said:

> **And saying, Sirs, why do ye these things? We also are men of like passions with you, and preach unto you that ye should turn from these vanities unto the living God, which made heaven, and earth, and the sea, and all things that are therein:**
> **—Acts 14:15**

The enemy will tell you you're so much better looking than everybody else; you are much more spiritual. But these lies are a trap! Yes, you're wonderful, but don't get carried away. Turn your eyes toward Jesus because he's the giver of any goodness you possess.

Satan doesn't leave because you yell at him. He goes when there is the power of faith behind what you say.

35

ROUND-UP

Let me give you a hot sheet of the devil's other tactics:

- **He tries to cast doubt over God's integrity and character.**

  By thy servants hast thou reproached the Lord....
  — Isaiah 37:24a

- **He tries to sabotage the positive progress of people to whom you have ministered.**
  In Acts 13 and 17, Satan persuaded the Jews to agitate crowds to turn people away from the Gospel. In Acts 15 he tried to trap new believers into legalism.

- **He works when the leaves are tender and the shoots are green—before the root system is well developed.**
  That's why it's important to pray for every person who comes to Jesus. You don't want the enemy to hinder any positive progress as the Lord works in their life. Charles Finney had an eighty percent retention rate of converts under his ministry—a phenomenal number. Nowadays the national average is around four percent. What was Finney's secret? He prayed for every single new convert.

- **He makes charges and accusations against you that he can't prove.**

> ...for the accuser of our brethren is cast down, which accused them before our God day and night.
> — Revelation 12:10b

- **He distracts you from Bible reading and prayer.**

I knew a young man who was excited about the Lord, sharing his faith, and getting people filled with the Holy Spirit. One day he came to me and said, "I'm going to quit reading the Bible and praying for a while. I need to take a break." It's been seven years, and he is still on break. Once you quit, it's hard to get back into the discipline of reading the Word, praying, and going to church.

- **He'll twist your words.**

David said:

> Every day they wrest my words: all their thoughts are against me for evil.
> —Psalm 56:5

- **He motivates people to write insulting, incriminating untruths about you.**

In Ezra 4:11–12, the Jew's enemies sent a letter to King Artaxerxes to incriminate them when their building program was only half done. It also happened to Nehemiah (Nehemiah 6). It will happen to anyone in the ministry.

I got a letter from a man who called me a no-good, tongue-talking, spirit-casting Hollywood entertainer. I sent him a thank you note and our newsletter, and I got a package in the mail—our newsletter torn in little pieces!

- **He tries to silence you when you ask for blessings.**

Blind Bartimaeus called out, "Jesus, Son of David, have mercy on me." The disciples said, "Quiet down. He hasn't got time for you." But Bartimaeus shouted all the louder and got what he was after (Luke 18). Don't let anybody quiet you down when you're asking something from Jesus.

Once, I talked to a man who believed God would provide him with a Boeing 747 so he could take young people on mission trips. Even though I thought it was a long shot, I encouraged him. I don't want to shoot down a dream that may come from God.

- **He tries to steal God's Word out of your heart.**

The parable of the sower says the devil tries to pluck the Word out of your heart (Luke 8:12). You might leave church and not remember what was preached. Take notes and review your notes within eight hours and that will help you to remember. You'll have a much better retention rate than the person who doesn't.

- **He tempts your flesh after you have experienced great success.**

In John 6:15 people wanted to set Jesus up as an earthly king. It always happens. You're tempted after having a great success. That's why Jesus fled the crowd and got alone to pray.

> Then those men, when they had seen the miracle that Jesus did, said, "This is of a truth that prophet that should come into the world."
> When Jesus therefore perceived that they would come and take him by force, to make him a king, he departed again into a mountain himself alone.
> —John 6:14–15

- **He tries to get you to use spiritual gifts in the wrong way or at the wrong time.**

One of the important things to learn about spiritual gifts is how to exercise them at the right time, in the right way.

241

My dad bought me a bike when I was a kid and said he didn't want me riding over curbs or on busy streets. When he wasn't looking, I'd go over curbs and on busy streets and through mud puddles. The gift was mine, but I chose to use it in the wrong way.

Likewise, spiritual gifts can be misused. You must have wisdom to know when it is the right time or the right manner in which to exercise your gift.

- **He tries to haunt you with the past.**

> **An ungodly man diggeth up evil: and in his lips there is as a burning fire.**
> **—Proverbs 16:27**

Paul wrote:

> **Brethren, I count not myself to have apprehended: but this one thing I do, forgetting those things which are behind, and reaching forth unto those things which are before,**
> **I press toward the mark for the prize of the high calling of God in Christ Jesus.**
> **—Philippians 3:13–14**

So you've had failures in the past. Haven't we all? It's over! Just get on with the program and press toward the mark of the prize of the high calling of Christ Jesus. Forget the past, and don't be haunted by it.

- **He tries to stir up your hurts and keep you bitter, unforgiving, and in the hands of the tormenter.**

Read the chilling parable in Matthew 18:23–35 and see how serious the offense of harboring an unforgiving attitude is. It can literally mean a death sentence.

- **If he can't get at you any other way, he'll try to attack you from within.**

Nehemiah discovered his enemies were inside the Jerusalem wall, claiming to be on his team. The early church was very good at recognizing and expelling those who tried to join them with wrong motives. When Simon the Sorcerer tried to hook up with them, Peter rebuked him harshly.

> **Repent therefore of this thy wickedness, and pray God, if perhaps the thought of thine heart may be forgiven thee.**
>
> —Acts 8:22

The devil may try to insert someone into your life who's an adversary posing as a friend, but the Holy Spirit will give you wisdom to discern their motives.

THREE SIMPLE IDENTIFIERS

Here are three ways to recognize an attack from the enemy.

1. His suggestions come to your mind, not your spirit.

If you are a born-again believer, Satan can never speak to your spirit. You will never receive deep revelation from him there. The things you know deep down in your "knower," where only the Lord speaks to you, come from God. The Holy Spirit is welded to your spirit, but the devil speaks to your mind.

2. His suggestions try to force you to take immediate action on an issue when it is not completely settled in your spirit.

A man called me once and said, "I've got a wife and four kids, and I've just quit my job. I'm coming to work for you. The Lord told me to." He seemed like a nice man, but I didn't feel settled in my spirit about the idea of him quitting his job with a wife and four kids. I felt pressured. Nonetheless, I called him back and told him I wouldn't hire him. I didn't want to be unkind, but at the same time I couldn't condone his presumption.

3. When Satan is involved, confusion will reign in your mind.

Sometimes your mind will be paralyzed. Luther said not to argue with the devil because he's had more than five thousand years of experience at confusion and misdirection. Just put your trust in Jesus and follow the principles you learn in the Word of God.

GET RID OF HIM!

If we're not to argue with the devil, what do we do? Cast him out! How?

1. Make sure you have your authority from Jesus, and be filled with the Spirit.

> Behold, I give unto you power to tread on serpents and scorpions, and over all the power of the enemy: and nothing shall by any means hurt you.
> —Luke 10:19

2. Build dynamic faith.

Don't be wishy-washy. Satan doesn't leave because you yell at him. He goes when there is the power of faith behind what you say.

3. Learn how to pray effectively.

Prayer is, one of the most powerful weapons we have in our arsenal. Ephesians 6 says to pray with all prayer and supplication. We receive instructions, answers, and divine energy in prayer.

4. Add action to your faith.

Don't just pray—do!

*We must recognize the enemy's tactics and
resist the devil by actively combating
the forces of darkness with
weapons that are from
God not this world.*

36

SPIRITUAL WARFARE
PRAYING

Have you reached a barrier you can't seem to break through? Do you find yourself up against a brick wall? Are you facing stubborn challenges that won't yield? Maybe it's time for spiritual warfare praying.

It's possible to combat the forces of darkness through prayer. The disciples saw how effective prayer was in Jesus' ministry. Here was a man who spoke to demons and they fled. He even spoke to the wind and the waves and they obeyed. And you and I can do the same.

Spiritual warfare is a hot topic, and much of the teaching on spiritual warfare is excellent and healthy. However, some teaching is on the outer edge of sanity. C. S. Lewis said there are two equal and opposite errors concerning the devil and warfare. The first is to deny or ignore his existence. The second is to credit him with too much power.

WHAT WARFARE PRAYING IS NOT

It's not making weird noises, screaming, or some type of spiritual "voodoo." This is how the false prophets of Baal acted. They screeched and screamed and waved their arms and cut themselves (1 Kings 18). That's not spiritual warfare.

It's not going to the top of the highest building in your city so you can get closer to the "principalities" and do real battle. Some people teach this, and say if there's not a tall building you need to rent a helicopter. However, that is *not* spiritual warfare!

It's not to presumptuously seek out a confrontation with the devil. When Jesus was led into the wilderness to be tempted by the devil, the Spirit led him. (Matthew 4:1). He didn't go looking for the devil, but He was not afraid to confront him.

What is spiritual warfare praying?

It's realizing we're in a war! We must recognize the enemy's tactics and resist the devil by actively combating the forces of darkness with weapons that are from God not this world.

SHOULD I PRAY WARFARE PRAYERS?

Yes! Let me give you seven quick reasons why.

1. Because victories are always won first in the spirit realm.

2. The source of trouble is most always spiritual forces of wickedness.

When you have trouble, the real source is not something you can see. Drugs are a problem, but not the source. Pornography is a problem, but not the source. Until we deal with the root, the symptoms will not leave. Spiritual victories must be won in the spirit.

3. It brings authentic revival to the church.

In his lectures on revival, Charles Finney said, "This is one of the first steps to authentic revival: realizing the authority in Christ we have over the devil and his forces of darkness."

Jesus said:

> Behold, I give unto you power to tread on serpents and scorpions, and over all the power of the enemy: and nothing shall by any means hurt you.
> —Luke 10:19

God didn't save us so we could sit around waiting to go to Heaven. He saved us so we could instigate revival—true life coming to the Church and the world!

4. It advances God's Kingdom on the earth.

We can actively take away the ground the devil has occupied and turn it into property for God's work. I love reading about the revivals of Israel, when they took the temples of Baal and turned them into public toilets. I'm happy to see adult bookstores turned into Christian bookstores. Displace the enemy and bring in the Kingdom of God.

Years ago, when I first became pastor, people told me not to expect a big revival in Lansing because there was a Samson spirit here. I didn't know what a Samson spirit was. Somebody else told me we were in the post-Christian era. I thought, "I'm a Christian and I'm still around. There's nothing 'post' Christian about me." But the one that topped them all was a man who said, "Because Lansing is the capitol city of Michigan, there are too many political demons around for us to have revival."

Our church started meeting for prayer on Thursday nights, and we laid out a map of the city and prayed over it. We prayed for the governor, the mayor, and the legislature. We prayed that God would expose all dishonesty in government. We prayed that God would bless those leaders with wisdom. We weren't afraid of so-called political demons. We had the Holy Spirit!

In 1987 the mayor gave me (on behalf of our church) the key to the city. In 1988 the state legislature wrote up a resolution honoring our church, and me, for having the most significant spiritual influence in Michigan. In 1989 the mayor made me the Grand Marshal of the Memorial Day parade. Mary Jo and I hopped into a convertible and rode through the city, waving at the thousands of people in the parade. I looked behind the car and there were the senators and legislators walking behind us.

There's no excuse for not advancing God's kingdom, and that's why we pray spiritual prayers of warfare.

5. It provides deliverance from evil.

Acts 10:38 says Jesus was anointed by the Holy Spirit and power, and went about doing good and healing all who were oppressed by the devil.

Ruby had an incurable eye disease and was going blind. Somebody told her about Mount Hope Church, so she came and received spiritual warfare prayer. An elder anointed her with oil and prayed, and Ruby's eyesight was restored. She told me about it. I was skeptical, so I told her to get a letter from her doctor. The next week she had a letter from her doctor. It explained her condition and said, "Now the condition affecting her vision is completely gone. Pastor Williams, this is nothing short of a miracle."

God will deliver us from evil when we believe He'll deliver us from evil. We must not think every bad thing is from God. If it kills, destroys, or steals it's not God, it's the devil, so actively fight against it.

> The thief cometh not, but for to steal, and to kill, and to destroy: I am come that they might have life, and that they might have it more abundantly.
>
> —John 10:10

6. We should pray spiritual warfare prayers to provide advance protection for the Church.

Let me share a little more about a crisis time in my life and ministry when spiritual warfare praying pulled me through.

My dream for Mount Hope Church has always been found in Acts 13:44:

> **And the next sabbath day came almost the whole city together to hear the word of God.**

I want our church to keep growing until the whole city comes to Christ. At one point we were worshiping in a 500 seat church and having five Sunday services. We needed a new facility, so in 1984 we launched the dream of a 3,000 seat worship center with a large facility for teaching, training, and praying. Our building committee agreed not to start until we had one million dollars in cash.

Then, some people in the construction business said, "Pastor, we're getting anxious. The property's sitting over there idle. Could we lay the foundation ourselves?" I knew we'd said we wouldn't lay any brick until we had a million dollars in cash, but they convinced me that the rest of the money would come when the people saw action, so I agreed.

They excavated and put the foundation in, but I had a very bad feeling about it so I put the project on hold, thereby angering the people who supported construction. They said I would be the laughingstock of the city. I said I couldn't help it—I had to obey God. Rumors circulated against me. The situation was increasingly stressful. Weeds were growing on the property and these people fought me and stirred up trouble. We needed a million dollars and all we had was around $35,000, so I just gave it to missions as an offering.

THREE VISIONS

I went to Chicago for a seminar and something happened to me that never happened before or since. As I lay on my bed in my hotel room, praying in the Spirit, I was caught up to another world. I hovered between the sky and the earth. I looked down and I saw our 500-seat church full of people. I saw a hideous creature holding a net and a weird sword over our city. Tens of thousands of people were squirming around inside the net, but this demon wouldn't let them go no matter how much I told him to. I looked down into the church and saw myself on the platform encouraging the people and saying, "We need to do spiritual warfare."

At that time, I knew nothing about spiritual warfare, but I said to the congregation, "Lift up your hands to fight." Then, simultaneously we shouted, "Principalities, rulers of darkness over Lansing, in the name of Jesus Christ, and by his shed blood, loose the people!" It was as if invisible angels were loosed against that dark spiritual power. The demon's net started to unravel. People began to fall down into our church.

Suddenly I was back in my hotel room. Less than a minute had passed. My heart was pounding, but I thought I just had a weird dream, so I lay back down and was caught up once again.

This time I was in a hospital delivery room with a woman who lay on the birthing table. I knew the woman represented Mount Hope Church. I was at her shoulder saying, "Push!" I have never seen anyone in such intense labor; her body suffered contractions and convulsions. Finally, a baby came out and a nurse took it. Then, another baby came out, and another. Babies started shooting out of this woman on the table. There were hardly enough nurses to care for them!

Suddenly, I was back in my hotel room. I felt like I had been in that birthing room for hours, but virtually no time had passed. I looked at my watch and no time had gone by at all. I lay down once more and was caught up for the third and final time.

I was somehow traveling through the sky. I landed on a corner of our new property, a vacant lot filled with weeds. For the first time, a voice spoke saying, "David, look what I'm doing." I knew it was God's voice. There was so much love and kindness in it, but I was angry. "I'm not going to look," I pouted. "All I want is to obey you. I put the project on hold, and now I'm the laughingstock of the city. My friends have left me; people have transferred their membership. I've had nothing but trouble and I'm not going to look."

The voice said nothing, but I could hear the sound of a truck coming down the road. The voice said again, "David, look what I'm doing." I finally obeyed and, to my surprise, I saw the church three-quarters of the way finished. I saw the plastic hanging over the entrance ways; there were bags of cement on the ground covered with plastic and bricks. I exclaimed, "God, you're doing it!"

Once again, I was back in my hotel room, excitement running through my soul. Again, not a second had passed. I wondered if I was going crazy. I told my wife about the experience, and after her encouragement, the next Sunday I told the church.

I called everyone to twenty-one days of spiritual warfare and fasting based on the experience of the prophet Daniel who prayed for twenty-one days to get a breakthrough (Daniel 10). One hundred people left the church, but altar calls tripled in size. Miraculous events intensified. God's presence and anointing grew stronger, and there was no dip in attendance or finances, even though 100 people had left the church. In fact, we were growing!

Three months later, my administrator ran into my office and told me we had a million dollars cash! People had donated houses they couldn't sell, and we were able to sell them overnight.

Not only that, when we started building the builders noticed that the wrong concrete was used in the original foundation—a lower grade than was necessary. Had we built on that foundation, the building would have collapsed within two years. God protected us through spiritual warfare praying.

7. Finally, we should engage in spiritual warfare praying simply because Jesus did it, so we must, too.

*The devil is under Jesus' feet, and even
if you and I are just his little toe,
the devil is still under us.*

37

PRAYER WARRIOR TRAINING

SIX STEPS TO GETTING STARTED

1. Always begin from a position of victory.

We're seated in heavenly places with Christ, far above all principalities and powers (Ephesians 2:6). The devil is under Jesus' feet, and even if you and I are just his little toe, the devil is still under us.

2. Don't wait for a special "burden" to get involved in spiritual warfare.

The Bible doesn't say "if you pray," it says "when you pray." When coupled with faith, prayer is the single most powerful activity a Christian can engage in. Pray regularly!

3. Remember our weapons are not of this world.

They are nuclear warheads compared to the devil's flyswatters. His armaments are limited to carnal weapons. We have supernatural ones.

> For though we walk in the flesh, we do not war after the flesh:
> (For the weapons of our warfare are not carnal, but mighty through God to the pulling down of strong holds;)

> Casting down imaginations, and every high
> thing that exalteth itself against the knowledge of
> God, and bringing into captivity every thought to
> the obedience of Christ....
> —2 Corinthians 10:3–5

4. Speak to the problem.

The spiritual roots of problems must listen and obey. When Jesus spoke to the fig tree, there was no immediate result, but a few days later it had withered from the roots (Mark 11). Roots will obey when you speak to them in Jesus' name.

5. Don't think it takes great amounts of time.

Warfare praying just takes a portion of your regular prayer life. A young man sat in the pew after a service. He was the last one in the sanctuary. I asked if he would like to accept Christ, and he said, "I can't. Something's holding me back." I placed my hand on his head and said, "In the Name of Jesus, devil, you loose this man's will."

The man started screaming and gagging. Mary Jo and the kids ducked for cover because they didn't know what was happening. Then he began to cry and accepted Christ. Later, he went home and got rid of all his satanic music and drug paraphernalia. Today, he is still a member of Mount Hope Church, and that all happened 25 years ago.

Short prayers can be powerful. In Acts 4, the disciples prayed a short prayer, and when they finished the building shook. Get a few committed believers to agree in prayer with you, and you'll be able to spiritually shake your city!

6. Use the sword of the Spirit—the spoken Word of God.

When Satan confronted him, Jesus said, "It is written." Then Jesus spoke a bite-sized portion of Scripture in context and it was enough to scare the devil off (Matthew 4:4).

Have you reached a roadblock and can't seem to break through? Spiritual warfare praying is your answer!

The church needs to come to a full revelation of the power we have in the Name of Jesus.

CONCLUSION

YOUR AUTHORITY AS A CHRISTIAN

The biblical truths we've covered in this book hold enough power to permanently thwart the enemy's plan for you, your spouse, your children, and your friends. You don't have to take it when the devil bullies you. You have authority over him. You can tell *him* what to do!

> But we see Jesus, who was made a little lower than the angels for the suffering of death, crowned with glory and honour; that he by the grace of God should taste death for every man....
> Forasmuch then as the children are partakers of flesh and blood, he also himself likewise took part of the same; that through death he might destroy him that had the power of death, that is, the devil;
> And deliver them who through fear of death were all their lifetime subject to bondage.
> —Hebrews 2:9, 14–15

The enemy has no more legal authority over the earth. Jesus holds the keys to hell and stripped away the devil's power. The only way the enemy can kill and destroy is if we allow him to deceive us into giving him the authority God meant for us.

When I was in high school, I went on a field trip and watched people slaughter chickens. I felt so sorry for the chickens because they would run around for awhile without any heads. That's what the devil is doing now. His power has been destroyed, but he's still running around trying to find somebody naive enough to dupe. You can crush a snake's head, but the body will still whip around. Jesus crushed Satan's head, but his body is still whipping around, taking people down with him.

Whenever I preach on spiritual warfare, strange things happen. My young daughter would have night terrors; my brakes would fail; I would lose my sermon notes. However, even though Satan's emissaries worked hard to frustrate me, God dispatched more angels to surround me. His angels surround his people and minister to those who are heirs of his salvation.

> **For he shall give his angels charge over thee, to keep thee in all thy ways.**
> —Psalm 91:11

> **For the angel of the Lord is a guard; he surrounds and defends all who fear him.**
> —Psalm 34:7 (NLT)

> **Are they not all ministering spirits, sent forth to minister for them who shall be heirs of salvation?**
> —Hebrews 1:14

"Ten-Four"

> **For the weapons of our warfare are not carnal, but mighty through God to the pulling down of strong holds....**
> —2 Corinthians 10:4

I call that the "10:4" verse. When the devil comes after you, say, "Ten-four devil—you're over and out! You have been demolished." When Jesus sent out seventy lay ministers to preach the Gospel, heal the sick, cleanse the leper, cast out devils, and even raise the dead he gave them the authority to do those things just as he gives us the authority now.

> And the seventy returned again with joy, saying, Lord, even the devils are subject unto us through thy name.
>
> —Luke 10:17

A leading cause of defeat among Christians is not realizing our authority in the Name of Jesus. We've mentioned it throughout this book, but it's a vitally important fact to keep in mind.

> And he said unto them, I beheld Satan as lightning fall from heaven.
>
> Behold, I give unto you power to tread on serpents and scorpions, and over all the power of the enemy: and nothing shall by any means hurt you.
>
> Notwithstanding in this rejoice not, that the spirits are subject unto you; but rather rejoice, because your names are written in heaven.
>
> —Luke 10:18–20

When you identify the enemy trying to wreck your life, take your God-given authority and cast him out. If he comes into your marriage or your family, cast him out. If he comes into your financial affairs, cast him out. God knows you face battles; he knows Satan is out to destroy you, but he has provided a way to triumph, and he will equip you to fight.

> Bless the Lord, who is my rock. He gives me strength for war and skill for battle.

> He is my loving ally and my fortress, my tower
> of safety, my deliverer. He stands before me as a
> shield, and I take refuge in him.
> —Psalm 144:1–2a (NLT)

All Satan's ability is carnal in nature. He must operate through people. But the weapons of our warfare are of faith. We've got the weapons of the Holy Spirit and the Name of Jesus! We've got the weapons of the Word of God and intercessory prayer. The church needs to come to a full revelation of the power we have in the Name of Jesus. Then we can win this war against our enemy and his generals, against their tactics and meddling. We can take back all that he stole and one day declare the final victory with Jesus over the devil.

What a glorious day that will be!

About Dave Williams, D. Min.

Dr. Dave Williams is pastor of Mount Hope Church and International Outreach Ministries with headquarters in Lansing, Michigan. He has pastored there for almost 30 years, leading the church from 226 members to over 4,000 today.

The ministry campus comprises 60 acres in Delta Township, Michigan, and includes a worship center, Bible Training Institute, children's center, youth and young adult facilities, Prayer Chapel, Global Prayer Center, Gym and Fitness Center, Care facilities, and a medical complex.

Construction of Gilead Healing Center was completed in 2003. This multi-million dollar edifice includes medical facilities, nutritional education, and fitness training. Its most important mission is to equip believers to minister to the sick as Jesus and his disciples did. Medical and osteopathic doctors, doctors of chiropractic and naturopathy, and licensed physical and massage therapists all work harmoniously with trained prayer partners to bring about miraculous healing for sick people from all over the United States.

Under Dave's leadership, 43 daughter and branch churches have been successfully planted in Michigan, the Philippines, Ghana, Ivory Coast, and Zimbabwe. Including all branch churches, Mount Hope Churches claim over 14,000 members.

Dave is founder and president of Mount Hope Bible Training Institute, a fully accredited, church-based leadership institute for training ministers, church planters, and lay people to perform the work of the ministry. Dave also established the Dave Williams' School for Church Planters, located in St. Pete Beach, Florida.

He has authored more than 60 books including bestseller, *The New Life...The Start of Something Wonderful* (with over 2 million books sold in eight languages). More recently, he wrote *The World Beyond: The Mysteries of Heaven and How to Get There* (over 100,000 copies sold). *Radical Riches* was a Barnes and Noble top seller for ten consecutive months. His *Miracle Results of Fasting* (Harrison House Publishers) was an Amazon.com five-star top seller for two years in a row.

Dave's articles and reviews have appeared in national magazines such as *Advance, Pentecostal Evangel, Charisma, Ministries Today, Lansing Magazine, Detroit Free Press, World News*, and others.

Dave has appeared on television in the United States and Canada, and has been heard worldwide over "The Hour of Decision," the weekly radio ministry of the Billy Graham Evangelistic Association. Dave's Sunday messages are available for download at www.mounthopechurch.org.

Along with his wife, Mary Jo, Dave established The Dave and Mary Jo Williams Charitable Mission (Strategic Global Mission), a non-profit foundation providing scholarships to pioneer pastors and ministry students, as well as grants to inner-city children's ministries.

CONTACT INFORMATION

Mount Hope Church and International Outreach Ministries
202 S. Creyts Road
Lansing, Michigan 48917

For a complete list of Dave Williams' life-changing
books, CDs and videos call:

Phone: 517-321-2780
800-888-7284
TDD: 517-321-8200

or go to our web site:
www.mounthopechurch.org

For prayer requests, call the
Mount Hope Global Prayer Center
24-hour prayer line at:
517-327-PRAY
(517-327-7729)

3 LIFE-CHANGING BOOKS
BY DAVE WILLIAMS

EMERGING LEADERS—They are wall breakers and city takers! Don't try to stop them. They are unstoppable. Don't try to understand them. They are often unorthodox in their approach. They are . . . EMERGING LEADERS—a new breed of church leadership for the 21st century, and you can be one of them! $12.⁹⁵

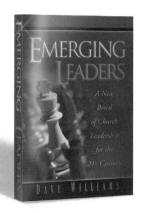

PRIVATE GARDEN—In this book Pastor Dave Williams shares encouraging prophetic words the Holy Spirit has spoken into his life and ministry. As you read, you will receive Holy Spirit encouragement and direction.

$12.⁹⁵

COMING INTO THE WEALTHY PLACE— God wants you to be able to "abound to every good work." You need to learn how to release God's power in your life to get wealth. This book will show you how to go through the door of just good enough into *The Wealthy Place!* $14.⁹⁵

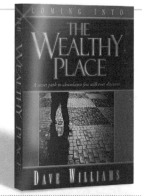

TO ORDER, CALL 1-800-888-7284, OR VISIT US ON THE WEB AT: WWW.MOUNTHOPECHURCH.ORG